Knitting

into the

Mystery

SUSAN S. JORGENSEN ✦ SUSAN S. IZARD

Knitting
into the
Mystery

A GUIDE TO THE SHAWL-KNITTING MINISTRY

MOREHOUSE PUBLISHING

Copyright © 2003 by Susan S. Izard and Susan S. Jorgensen

Morehouse Publishing
P.O. Box 1321
Harrisburg, PA 17105

Morehouse Publishing is an imprint of Church Publishing, Inc.

Credits are on page 144.

Library of Congress Cataloging-in-Publication Data
Jorgensen, Susan S., 1951–
  Knitting into the mystery : a guide to the shawl-knitting ministry /
Susan S. Jorgensen, Susan S. Izard.
      p.cm.
Includes bibliographical references.
  ISBN 0-8192-1967-3
  1. Prayer. 2. Knitting—Religious aspects—Christianity. I. Izard, Susan S., 1957– II. Title.
  BV215.J68 2003
  247—dc21

                                                                  2003005088

Printed in the Malaysia
06 07 08 10 9 8

DEDICATION

for Janet Bristow and Victoria A. Cole-Galo
whose vision began this ministry in 1998

for our grandmothers
who taught us to knit

for Jordan
who was the inspiration for this particular book

and for knitters everywhere
may their knitting be their praying
may their praying draw them more deeply into the Mystery we call God

CONTENTS

You formed my inmost being;
you knit me in my mother's womb.
—PSALMS 139:13

Celebrations

Patricia Loring introduces her book, *Listening Spirituality: Personal Spiritual Practices Among Friends* in the following way: "Most books have a page of acknowledgments. I want this book to have pages of *Celebrations*. I'm celebrating the unique, God-given giftedness of many people; and I'm celebrating the generous gifts they have made of their abilities, time and energy . . ."[1] We couldn't agree with her more. Throughout our lives, God calls us to celebrate the miracle of each person, each day, each seeming "coincidence" through which the daily rhythms of our life unfold.

Susan S. Izard celebrates:

—Myra Bowers, who gave her the shawl she uses in the Quiet Room. This shawl inspired the two of them to begin the shawl-knitting ministry at their church.

—all the knitters at her church who have given countless hours to knitting the shawls that have comforted and nurtured so many people. Without their generous hearts and loving spirits, this ministry would not have happened.

—Cathy Murtha, DW, who wrote the first prayers of healing and comfort that accompanied the shawls. Through Cathy's loving spirit, Susan and her knitting circle discovered that praying with and for others was as meaningful as the shawls that they gave away.

—her family: her husband, Bob; her children, Catherine, Thomas, and Margaret, who have filled her life with love. She celebrates her mother, Anne, who encouraged her to be creative; and her four sisters, Sally, Kitty, Amey, and Carrie, who grew up knitting with her. She celebrates the spirit of her father, Newt, who taught her the importance of caring for others.

Susan S. Jorgensen celebrates:

— the people for whom she has knit a shawl; the grace that each has brought her has been humbling and profound.

—her beloved friends who have supported her faithfully, taught her patiently, loved her dearly, and laughed and cried with her when she needed them the most.

—her grandmother, Mildred Clara Holway, who loved her unconditionally.

—her family: her husband, Jorg; her children, Amy, Matthew, and Stacy. She has come to know God's steadfast love, humor, and passion through their presence in her life.

Together, we celebrate the Spirit of the ministry, who has been our muse, who has encouraged us when we were at a loss for words, and who has blessed our time together.

And finally, we celebrate our God who knits us into wholeness, who enables us to care for others, who encircles the world in an eternal shawl of love and compassion. We celebrate our God who is Presence, who is Wisdom, who is Mystery.

PART ONE

IN THE
BEGINNING

CHAPTER 1
INTRODUCTION

Susan S. Jorgensen

Behold, I am doing a new thing;
now it springs forth, do you not perceive it?

—ISAIAH 43:19 RSV

Sit down with a group of knitters anywhere and ask them to tell you stories about how they learned to knit. Many of the stories are humorous; some are tender; some are gently self-deprecating. Nearly all are colored with a love or fascination for knitting; nearly all reveal relationships with at least one other person, the person who taught them how. I have laughed out loud at some of the tales and been teary-eyed at others. For many reasons, people today are expressing a renewed interest in the ancient art of knitting—articles and work-shops about it have become commonplace. This shawl-knitting ministry is a part of that resurgence. Let me begin at the beginning of my own story.

Now as I knit . . .
I think of two
people . . .
the person
I am knitting . . .
for and my
grandmother—
for all the gifts she
had given me.[2]

Elliott Kronenfeld

On my eighth birthday, my grandmother gave me a pair of bright blue metal knitting needles and a skein of blue-and-white variegated yarn. With her own two hands that were quite gnarled with arthritis even then, she taught me how to knit and purl. And while that happened over four decades ago, it is also as if it occurred yesterday. Her hands were like no one else's that my young eyes had ever seen. Many strange odd-shaped age spots dotted the backs of her hands and her veins were very pronounced; the skin on her crooked fingers seemed thin and appeared shiny. All the joints of her fingers were swollen and looked sore. She never complained. One of the clearest snapshots that I have in my own memory banks is of my grandmother's hands confidently holding her knitting needles as the yarn snaked around her fingers in a very particular way so that the tension was just so.

I knit and unraveled that skein of yarn at least a dozen times, always striving for fewer mistakes—fewer holes, fewer "extra" stitches, less areas that looked moth-eaten and ragged. The yarn frayed and grew somewhat ratty and gray from all the tugging of my awkward fingers. But after a while, the needles stopped feeling like foreign objects of unknown origin in my little hands and I got the hang of it. Eventually, I graduated to finishing rectangles of various sizes that I turned into capes and skirts for my dolls, adding snaps as closures, elastic for waistbands, and bits of rickrack for trim.

My "gram" was left-handed, and so for nearly a dozen years I purled backwards, doing it faithfully the way she had taught me. Don't ask me how I did it; I only know that I purled that way until I sought help with a sweater from an expert knitter on my dorm floor during my freshman year of college. She insisted that I must have been knitting some intricate, complex stitch. I adamantly denied this. We went back and forth as I continued to tell her that I was doing the stockinette stitch—knit one row, purl one row—just the way my grandmother had taught me. She finally invited me to sit down and show her exactly what I was doing. After watching me carefully, she told me that I was purling backwards. I don't remember now how long it took me to relearn the stitch, but I lost a little of my gram in the transition. My stockinette stitch now looks just like the pictures in the knitting books; the strange little twist in every row is only a memory.

I knit for many years when my own three children were young. I knit sweaters and scarves for nearly every member of my family—crewnecks and cardigans, raglan sleeves and saddle shoulders, ribbing and baby cables. And when everyone had one, I knit my children's dolls sweaters to match their own. Knitting provided me with a creative outlet as an at-home mom. As the children grew and my own life became increasingly busy, I knit less and less until I had very few knitting projects in the works, and no plans for new ones. At one rare idle point, I picked up a half-done sweater I had begun knitting years before, thinking that I might really get around to finishing it. To my horror, I discovered that the expensive, cream-colored, somewhat exotic yarn was moth-eaten. With a sigh and a groan, I threw it away and pushed my yarn bag even further back in the front hall closet. I began to wonder if I would ever find the time to knit again.

And then, at the center where I have been an associate spiritual director for many years, I began to see people wearing and knitting shawls. The first shawl I saw captured my full attention because I couldn't figure out exactly how it was made—I wasn't even sure if it was knit or crocheted. The woman who was wearing it removed it from her shoulders so that I could look at it in detail. I was puzzled, awed, drawn. Even after the director of our center explained the

*Knitting is the
simplest and
most ordinary
of activities,
yet somehow it
mysteriously
contains within
itself the potential
for expanding
our conscious
awareness.*[3]

SUSAN GORDON LYDON

pattern to me, I had a hard time picking it out. It took my eyes a while before they could "see" what the yarn was doing.

That was it. I was hooked. Completely. Utterly. True confession: I felt completely preoccupied in the same way I felt when I first began to date my husband in the fall of our junior year in college. Trips to the store to buy yarn became prayer pilgrimages. My inventory of yarn grew; it felt like I was adding to the unwritten list of people who needed shawls almost daily. I purchased a lovely wide, deep woven basket to hold all the yarn. I couldn't go into a craft store without at least a flyby of the yarn section to see if any new skeins had been put on the shelves since my last visit. I fell hard for this "new" old love in my life.

I knit my first shawl in February of 2001 for a woman whose husband of six months had died in a car accident. While I knitted, I prayed to enter her grief; I prayed light into every stitch; I prayed that she be comforted; I prayed that she be healed. I prayed that she would come to see her grief as an expression of her love, that the two were inextricably bound, one to the other. I chose to knit the shawl with a yarn called "Adirondack" (named after a mountain range in the northeastern part of the United States), in part because I knew that they had loved the outdoors together and in part because the colors of gray and brown evoked for me the sense and mood of grieving.

Since then, I have knit shawls to celebrate friendship and connection; I have given shawls to people who are moving, to women who are getting married, to people who need physical and psychological healing, to people in transition, to my children just "because." I knit one shawl for two people—for a woman who was dying of cancer and her best friend. I did not know the woman who was dying of cancer, but I knew her friend.

I wanted to create a shawl that they could share as this woman lived out her last months, one that would then pass to my grieving friend. Sometimes my friend would tell me, "Pat has the shawl this week; it's been a tough week for her." At others, she would say, "I have the shawl now; it's just been hard to watch her suffer." My hope is that now that Pat has died, my friend finds comfort in the presence of her friend through her wearing of the shawl.

It is not unusual for me to have five or six shawls going at once. The need for them and the desire to knit them seem to be like a fire that feeds itself. As my heart opens more deeply, my awareness of people who would benefit from a shawl grows. Tragedy and illness are immediate needs; friendship and connection are needs that are less pressing. It is not unusual for me to put aside a celebration shawl for a period of time to knit one for a friend who has recently experienced the death of a loved one or just received the shattering diagnosis of cancer.

Susan and I have written this book for those who are already involved in this amazing outreach of love and compassion. We have also written it for beginners, a primer of sorts for the ministry. We have entitled it *Knitting into the Mystery* because that is how it feels to us. No matter how well crafted the words, no matter how articulate we might strive to be, part of the process of knitting shawls, giving them away, and receiving them will always be Mystery— something that lies just beyond our ability to describe or capture in words.

The word "mystery" comes from the Greek word *myein*, which literally means "to shut the eyes." This shawl-knitting ministry invites us to "shut our eyes" in order that we can be open to seeing what happens within ourselves and within the context of an encounter with "other." The mystery that unfolds silently in the rhythm of K3, P3 (knit three, purl three) asks us to risk seeing new things,

Let your worship and your service be a fresh miracle every day to you.[1]

BAAL SHEM TOV

to experience the divine in ways that may feel unconventional or unfamiliar. I am reminded of the verse from Isaiah 43:19 (RSV): "Behold, I am doing a new thing; now it springs forth, do you not perceive it?" God is *always* doing something new with and for and in us.

The strange and paradoxical thing that happens, however, as we allow ourselves to fall into this unseen Mystery, is that we then begin to see Mystery manifest itself visually: the invisible is made visible by the labor of our own hands. After the casting on and the knitting of the first few rows (which, to me, are an absolutely tedious part of the process), suddenly the rows begin to form something. Always the moment arrives when this odd jumble of stitches and rows emerges from its own unique chrysalis to reveal a beautiful pattern of color and texture. Even though this happens with every shawl I have knit, how and when the shawl actually begins to look like itself is always different. I am delighted by this magical experience every time it happens. Out of a single strand of yarn, a flowing fabric emerges that will eventually wrap itself around another's shoulders and speak love into another's heart, a visual expression of Mystery. No two shawls look or feel alike; similarly, I have yet to find two people who knit in exactly the same way. All of these things work together to express the inexpressible Mystery that is a steadfast presence in our lives—God, Sophia, Allah, Yahweh, Wisdom, Abba, Amma.

This book will be part instruction, a passing on of all that we have learned in the years that we have been involved in knitting shawls for others. It will be part reflection, as we attempt to put into words what actually happens when we knit, when we pray, when we gather, when we give away, when we receive. It will be part story, as we tell you what has happened to us and to many others who

It is by faith that we understand that the ages were created by a word from God, so that from the invisible the visible world came to be.

HEBREWS 11:3 NJB.

have been involved in this ministry. And it will be part prayer, as we pass on to you the prayers that we have written when we have given shawls away and that we have invited others to write specifically for this book.

Susan and I have both been raised within the Christian tradition; she is a United Church of Christ minister; I am a Roman Catholic laywoman. Recognizing that God can neither be contained nor expressed by any one tradition, our hope is to write in a way that is open to all traditions, faiths, and expressions. One way we have done this is to invite people from various faiths and traditions to contribute prayers to the book. We also ask you, our readers and knitters, to have patience with us when we fall prey to the conditioning and expressions of our own tradition.

CHAPTER 2

A HISTORY OF THE SHAWL-KNITTING MINISTRY

Susan S. Izard

Knitting, like drumming, is a feat of homegrown magic.[5]

—Susan Gordon Lydon

In the fall of 1999, a woman in my church knit me a prayer shawl to keep on my rocker in the Quiet Room, the place where I offer spiritual direction. I was delighted by this glorious, thick, cozy, off-white shawl. I draped it over the back of the rocking chair I use when giving spiritual direction. As I thanked her, we began to talk about the process of knitting the shawl.

She first heard of knitting shawls at the Hartford Seminary. The shawl-knitting ministry was created by Vicky Galo and Janet Bristow after they completed the Women's Leadership Institute. When they graduated, they were encouraged to carry on the spirit of the class through some kind of project.

During the Institute they encountered the empowerment and wisdom of the Divine Feminine. It was in that spirit that they felt called to knit shawls for new mothers and women with breast cancer. The word spread and other members of the class began knitting. Soon shawls were being knit for many purposes, including important celebrations.

The woman from my church heard about the knitting and decided to knit one for me. As we were talking, it occurred to us that we needed a shawl-knitting ministry at our church. We knew that many church members could benefit from a shawl, and we knew many women who would enjoy being part of a knitting circle. The knitting was simple. The supplies were easy to get. We made plans and announced our first meeting.

Ten women attended our first knitting circle one cold January morning in 2000. We gathered around a candle in rockers and wooden chairs with our knitting needles and yarn. Many of us had already begun to make shawls, having received the directions ahead of time; others were just getting started. The Quiet Room was abuzz with activity and excitement as we helped each other cast on, discussed the variety of colors being knitted, and experienced the joy of being together. Our opening prayer wrapped us in the compassion and love of the Holy One and grounded us in the purpose of our work—to knit God's love, care, and warmth into shawls for those who needed them.

The first meeting went so well that by February our circle had almost doubled. Something else happened, something that none of us had anticipated or expected. The story of the shawl-knitting ministry and the shawls began to unfold.

In January, we gave away our first shawls. By the February meeting, we were able to tell each other the stories about giving away the shawls. We read the

Be imitators of God, as beloved children, and live in love.

EPHESIANS 5:1

moving thank-you notes. One note read, "The prayer shawl is a treasure. I know it will warm my shoulders and my heart often as I think of the love that went into the knitting and that radiates out from it. I feel blessed." Another came from a woman diagnosed with cancer. "Thank you so much for your beautiful note and please extend my heartfelt thanks to the knitting ministry. I did not want to be a recipient of a 'prayer shawl' and was reluctant (at first) to take it. But as soon as I put it on, I felt the warmth and power of the prayers that went into it. It has not left me since—I even sleep with it. The shawl is absolutely beautiful and is helping me through this incredibly challenging time." Another woman, recently widowed, wrote, "Thank you for the lovely prayer shawl I received at my husband's Memorial [Service]. It has been a great comfort to me. The colors blend together beautifully just like your prayers as you knit. The shawl is on the back of my husband's favorite chair, which is close to my home's entrance. It is the last thing seen by me as I leave and the first when I enter. My home does not seem so empty and I feel God's love and arms around me."

Each story meant so much to us. The intimate notes touched us. We were amazed that a simple shawl could convey so much comfort and love. With each shawl we gave away, a note or story came back. Again and again we heard about the comfort the shawls provided. Gradually, the stories strengthened our faith; they became witnesses to God's compassion for God's people. We realized our knitting enabled people to encounter God's love in a tangible way. What our hands and hearts created allowed others to know God. Our knitting was linked to God's great creative energy that blankets us with compassion. Our work and care linked us to God's grace.

But a Samaritan traveler who came upon him was moved with compassion at the sight.

LUKE 10:33

Month after month we continued to meet, to knit, to pray, to talk with one another, and to bless the shawls. While discussing this ministry with one of the women who trained me to be a spiritual director, I discovered that she was also knitting shawls and had written prayers for the ministry. By the spring of 2000, we included the "Prayer for Healing," which you may find on page 116, as well as the "Prayer of the Mantle of Healing" with each shawl we gave away. Again, we were delighted to discover that the prayers were as important as the shawls. One woman, whose husband was dying, wrote, "With sincere gratitude we thank you for the lovely prayer shawl you knitted and prayed over for my husband, Phil. What a beautiful way to bring comfort and the security of the love of God. It is a part of our daily lives, and when Phil is in a lot of pain, he wants it wrapped around him. The 'Prayer for Healing' is beautiful and affirming. God is there for us, the many prayers from everyone give us strength, and with that we can get through our difficult times with grace. God bless you all."

During the first six months of knitting with the women at church, the shawl-knitting ministry became a way of praying for me. I discovered that knitting the shawls and praying into them was as important a time of contemplation and prayer as my morning prayer and meditation. After years of ordained ministry and studying theology, I was amazed by the simplicity of the shawl-knitting ministry. Like Susan, I was taught to knit by my grandmother. Simple knitting is natural for me. It is a part of who I am. Mixing knitting and ministry was new, however. I was struck by the contrast between my theological education, which valued intellectual achievement, and the power of the shawl-knitting ministry, which was an experience of a living God. What was ministry, really? Was it possible that all I needed to know was how to knit? Was it possible

Wisdom teaches us that arriving at the Truth is experiencing the graciousness and loving kindness of God.[6]

JOHN MAIN

that God was calling me to simple caring rather than to complex theological issues? It was clear that, through my knitting and the knitting of the women around me, God had engaged us in a great act of compassion. Our knitting was weaving us—our hearts and our souls—into the truth of God's love.

In the summer of 2000, I decided to write a biblical reflection on the shawl-knitting ministry using the text from Psalm 139:13–14 (NJB): "You created my inmost self, knit me together in my mother's womb. For so many marvels I thank you; a wonder am I, and all your works are wonders." The psalm describes God's intimate presence in the creation of our lives. It explains that God knows us even before our birth. It implies that God's creative energy knits us together in our mother's womb and is integral to our birth, life, and death. Conveying this love and the practical elements of the shawl-knitting ministry was the purpose of writing my article, "Knitting into the Mystery of God," which was published in the September 2000 issue of *Presence: The Journal of Spiritual Directors International.*

On a whim, I added my email address to the end of the article. This inspiration brought us to the next chapter of the shawl-knitting ministry. Much to my surprise, as soon as the article was published, I received email after email requesting more information with questions about how to create this ministry in various churches all over the world. Friends were photocopying the article for other friends. A grassroots shawl-knitting ministry movement had begun.

Month after month I read the emails and letters I received to those gathered at our shawl-knitting ministry meetings. We had fun listening to the stories and connecting with people from around the world. Once again, the shawl-knitting ministry was bringing the power of God into our lives. Something much greater than just knitting shawls was happening. God's compassion had a life of its own. By giving away the shawls and telling others about the ministry, we were swept up into God's energy without even knowing it was happening. It was delightful to watch love unfold, to laugh at the joy being shared, and to knit into the Mystery.

As I write in the winter of 2003, our shawl-knitting ministry has given away over 350 shawls to parishioners, friends, family members, and strangers halfway around the world. We have gathered with women from other knitting ministries in the area to hear the stories of their ministries—stories of healing, stories of caring for battered and homeless women, and stories of reaching out into the world to those in need. We have begun a project together knitting Peace Shawls for Afghanistan and have sent our first shipment off to the Afghan Women's Council. We now have pictures of Afghanistan women refugees wrapped in our shawls. We have also discovered an online community of shawl knitters that links us to people all over the world who have been touched by this ministry (see References, page 138). This book is an effort to continue the story, to share our ideas, and to invite men and women from all religious traditions to be a part of the life and ministry of knitting shawls.

CHAPTER 3
CONTEMPLATIVE KNITTING

Susan S. Jorgensen

The ultimate value of life depends upon awareness,
and the power of contemplation rather than upon mere survival.

—ARISTOTLE

Everyone seems to be knitting these days; it's *the* handicraft of the hour. What is the attraction of this ancient art? Knitting provides an antidote to the current chaos of modern day life. Its very nature helps us slow down and pay attention; its spirit invites contemplation.

The word *contemplation* has become a familiar, perhaps even overused word for those who follow a spiritual path. Seekers learn about it, practice it, long to master it. As a cradle Catholic, my first exposure to what I thought was contemplation were those dramatic storybook paintings of saints tied to the stake, their eyes gazing upward toward heaven. In my young mind and vivid imagination, contemplation was reserved for nuns and priests and truly holy people, and the more torture they endured, the better. Contemplation was definitely not for the faint of heart, and certainly not meant for ordinary folk.

Forty or so years later, I can tell you what contemplation is not. It is not reserved for saints. It isn't experienced only in a monk's cell or during deep, silent prayer. Ordinary folks like you and me experience it. And it seems to occur frequently and with ease in children. However, because contemplation leads us straight into the heart of Mystery, it is harder to put its meaning into words.

My favorite explanation of contemplative presence is Walter Burghardt's article, "Contemplation: A Long, Loving Look at the Real."[7] He wisely suggests that, in our search to be contemplative, we learn five things:

- how to inhabit the desert,
- how to develop a feeling of festivity,
- how to play,
- how to refrain from possessing the object of our delight,
- and how to make friends with people we know have taken a long and loving look at the real.

Burghardt's points speak to my own experience of contemplative presence in the middle of my knitting circle and in the quiet of my living room as I knit beside the fire on cold winter nights.

Inhabiting the Desert

Burghardt, a Jesuit priest, tells us that "the desert is not a place but an experience that takes hold of you, becomes part of you, turns you inside out."[9] In my

Knitting is a lovely rhythmic motion. It can soothe and calm you. It can even put you into a meditative trance. While your hands are busy, your mind can be emptied of anxieties and details.[8]

LISA R. MYERS

own experience, knitting helps us to do just that. Once we are beyond the beginning stages of knitting a shawl, when we must attend to every twist and turn of the yarn, taking care not to drop or add stitches—once the pattern becomes a part of us—then the knitting itself helps us to enter our own deserts. We notice things differently in these "places." Needless and seemingly endless distractions drift away and we are left with a sense of space and, in that space, a sense of stillness. As we rise into this silence, we fall into its Mystery. To our surprise and delight, we discover that the desert is not an uninhabitable geographic place, but an experience of unfathomable, unmistakable grace.

I experience this every time my own knitting circle gathers. Amidst the laughter and the stories, amidst the calls of "Help, I've dropped a stitch!" or "How do I weave in the end of the new skein?" and within the distinct sound of needles chattering together, the experience itself asserts itself, becomes "place," and seeps into the deeper corners of our being. It winds itself around the edges of our conversations and through our hearts, knitting itself into us. Our humble knitting circle takes hold of each of us, and we of it, and becomes a dwelling of spirit and joy. We know contemplative presence without expending effort or working at it. It is an organic experience and part of why I believe all serious knitters will tell you they are "hooked" by the craft.

Becoming Festive

The word "festive" is derived from the word "*feast*"; *Webster's Dictionary* defines it as "joyous and mirthful" (not words we hear often). Burghardt refers to Joseph Pieper, who describes festivity as "activity that is meaningful in itself."[10] How often are we imprisoned by the demands we make on ourselves to be productive? All the time. Our culture reinforces this value. We measure good days by the length of the list of tasks we have accomplished, and the more the better. Doing "nothing" doesn't make this list.

Whether I'm knitting alone or in my knitting circle, I've come to discover that knitting these shawls for others *is* an activity that is meaningful in itself. How else to explain the depth to which those of us who do it are captivated by it? When we knit, we don't have other things to bother about and we don't need to strain this way or that. Something happens. Time shifts as soon as our hands pick up the shawls we are knitting. Place becomes transparent. As the yarn circles our fingers and goes around our needles, the activity of watching our shawls grow stitch by stitch and row by row holds our attention captive; it seeks nothing but itself. Our minds are stilled by the flow of the yarn and the sound of our needles. And we are caught up in the festivity—the utter joy—of it all.

Learning to Play

Burghardt seems to anticipate his readers' objections to the word *play* when he tells us that he doesn't mean "fooling around."[11] He is talking about activity that sweeps us up into itself—watch children sitting on the floor with a set of Legos, notice how engrossed they become, how nothing else matters, how everything else slips away. This is play. Adults forget how to play, for lots of reasons. And when we try to play, we often turn it into deadly serious work that is fiercely competitive.

Burghardt tells us that play "demands a sense of wonder."[12] When my son was two and a half, his inquisitive mind and hands explored everything with zeal simply because it was there to explore. With his limited language skills, he would often lead us by the hand to the object that had most recently captured his attention and ask, "Why for?" Visiting friends in Vermont one winter, he knelt on the floor for hours by a swivel office-type chair and twirled it around

*Let the rivers
clap their hands,
the mountains
shout with them
for joy.*

PSALM 98:8

and around, his bright blue eyes looking intently at the mechanism responsible for its movement. Captivated, mesmerized, full of wonder, his play completely swept up his little being, and us—his silent observers—along with it. Matthew had encountered a desert as he became engrossed in playing with that chair; and we had been led into ours through our intense noticing of him.

Contemplative activity leads us into a complete engagement with two worlds—the seen and the unseen, the material and the spiritual, the world of time and place and the world that knows no time and has no limits. When we play, our minds are open to all dimensions of existence—we become fully awake, alert, and alive. Knitting is like that. When we pick up a set of knitting needles, we are drawn into that level of attention, sometimes without realizing it, and our play is just that—effortless, engaging, and full of wonder.

To Burghardt's understanding of the relationship between play and wonder, I would also add surprise as an important element of play. Watching a shawl grow long in my lap and gain substance always fills me with surprise. I could probably tell you that I have spent "x" number of hours knitting so far, and I usually know exactly who the shawl is for and why, so there is no real or obvious source for either the wonder or the surprise. And yet I am unable to take my eyes from the emerging garment; it draws me in; no matter how much I gaze, my inner eye whispers to my inner ear that there is yet more wonder and surprise to see, to absorb, in which to be delighted. While my outer eye sees a shawl emerging, my inner eye perceives a love, a stillness, and a deep peace that have neither limit nor end.

Letting Go

Burghardt describes this "letting go" as refraining from trying "to 'possess' the object of your delight."[14] Contemplative presence cannot be possessed; it can

My eye and God's eye are one and the same— one in seeing, one in knowing, one in loving.[13]

MEISTER ECKHART

only be appreciated. We can delight in it and celebrate it; be surprised and filled with joy by it. But we can't own it or create it or make it happen by willing it to be so. Contemplative presence is actually quite the opposite: it comes to us as surprise, to possess us gently, to capture us tenderly, to hold us dearly, revealing the One who is All.

Similarly, the shawls that we knit and receive seem to be on loan from some higher place. I look at the shawl that a very dear friend knit for me as it drapes casually over a favorite chair in my living room. I know that she knit it for me, and that it is mine. And yet neither of those things expresses the whole truth. Something more is at work in the shawls that we knit, something more than knit three, purl three. The totality of the shawl is more than the sum of the knitter, the wearer, and the yarn, and is something that we can't possess. Mystery invites us simply to attend to it, to relish in it, to savor the flow and the feel of yarn over fingers, of shawl over shoulders.

Making Friends

Walter Burghardt's last piece of advice to us about contemplation is to make friends with those who are contemplative. It seems to rub off on us, more something that we "catch" than do. His list of friends ranges from Abraham and Mary, to Rabbi Heschel, to Flannery O'Connor. Each knitter's list of people within whom they recognize a contemplative presence, whether it be a friend or a stranger, a living person or someone who has died, will be different. What is important here is to recognize how much we learn from the examples of others.

Friendship is also a necessary part of passing on the ancient art and prayer of knitting. While you may be one of the lucky ones who can look at a diagram and follow it with ease (I do better standing on my head and clapping my hands

*With grace,
the Holy Presence
is born into the
space that we make
by giving over
our own agendas:
God with us,
a third presence in
our encounter.[15]*

Patricia Loring

at the same time), it seems that it is much easier to pass on the art, one to another, in a face-to-face encounter. Much more transpires between teacher and pupil than the mere "how-to" of knitting. The bond created as we pass this craft on is like no other.

Recently, I was helping my two nieces, the older of whom is fifteen, the younger twelve, with scarves they were knitting. The twelve-year-old has a passion for it; she and I sat for quite a while as I showed her how to see her mistakes (she had two extra stitches on her needles) and how to pick up a stitch that had been dropped three rows back. I explained to her that her ability to knit depended upon her ability to look carefully (that "long, loving look at the real") and see what the yarn was doing.

She became very still and, while people in the kitchen were cleaning up after our holiday meal, stacking dishes, laughing, and just making noise in general, a holy hush began to build between her bent head and mine as we sat at the dining room table. The connection between us was palpable, real, whole, engaging—a friendship between generations, between two beings caught up in the love of knitting. The space between us filled with a presence that drew us together wordlessly, silently, deeply.

In the end, there seems to me to be a common thread running through all of these suggestions from Walter Burghardt. I believe the primary ingredient in contemplative presence is our heartfelt desire to live intentional lives, to be fully alive and awake in each moment. As a wise and seasoned spiritual guide once told me, "With God, there is always more to notice." Our knitting draws us in and creates a quiet where we are more alive and more capable of noticing, where we find ourselves in deserts that enchant us through the delicate bloom of yarn and needles and shawls that grow with each completed stitch and row.

Awake,
O sleeper,
and arise
from the dead.

EPHESIANS 5:14

PART TWO

CASTING ON

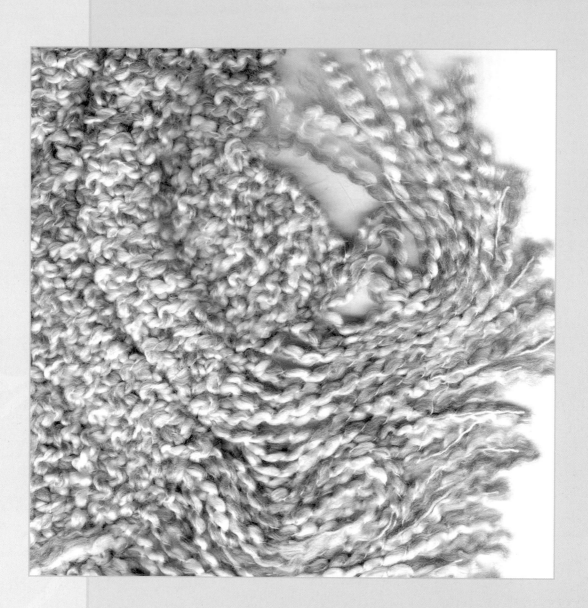

CHAPTER 4
OPENING YOUR HEART

Susan S. Izard

It is comforting to think that we may be of help
in ways that we don't even realize.[16]
—RACHEL NAOMI REMEN, M.D.

A few years ago I received an email from a man who had come across the shawl-knitting ministry at a local Spiritual Directors International meeting in Illinois. Shawls were displayed at the meeting. The man felt it was a perfect gift for his wife who had just been diagnosed with cancer. When he inquired how he could buy a shawl for her, he was told that they were not for sale and he needed to knit his own. Then he told me, "As a kid, my mother taught all her children to knit, both male and female. I have not taken up knitting needles in the last forty-plus years. The combination of the Spiritual Directors International meeting, your article, and my wife's cancer led me back

Each one of us matters, has a role to play, makes a difference. . . . Together we must reestablish our connections with the natural world and with the spiritual power that is around us.[17]

JANE GOODALL

So then you are no longer strangers and sojourners, but you are fellow citizens with the holy ones and members of the household of God.

EPHESIANS 2:19

to knitting. In a matter of three days, I knitted three skeins of wool. Since she has to receive her chemotherapy as an inpatient for four days at a time and she will have six hospitalizations in all, the prayer shawl has become a real blessing to her. I have since knitted four more shawls which are scattered throughout our home waiting for a person to choose them."

I loved receiving this email. It touched me deeply because it tells the story of the ministry so clearly. When we first discover the shawl-knitting ministry, we usually connect with it because we know someone who would benefit from a shawl. We find ourselves making mental notes of various people who are sick, mourning, or about to celebrate a big event, and we begin to knit for them. As we shop for the yarn, we think about what color might be best for the person. As we cast on the first stitches, we can begin to pray specifically for this person, naming them before God and asking God to wrap them in God's compassionate love. As we finish the shawl and add the fringe, we are still holding the person we are knitting for in our prayers. We are praying for God's embracing love to encompass the person.

By the time the person receives it, the shawl is filled with prayers for that individual. When they wrap themselves in it, they can feel the warmth and love that the prayers and yarn have become. Time after time we have received notes testifying to the remarkable comfort and compassion the recipients feel when they receive such a shawl, and expressing their gratitude. Sometimes people tell us that when they wear their shawls they feel a contentment and peace they've never before experienced.

While we often know the person who will receive our first shawl or shawls, there comes a time when we want to keep knitting shawls but don't know of anyone who needs one. If you're involved in a knitting circle at a church or in a community center, there is often a staff person who collects shawls to give to people who the community knows could use one. It is important to understand that, even though you might be knitting for an unknown person, the love and prayers that you knit into the shawl are just as powerful and important as they are for the shawls knit for specific individuals. This is a wonderful opportunity to pray for a stranger and to open your heart to God's love for the greater community and world. While knitting and praying for someone you don't know is a different experience than the intercessory prayers for a specific individual, praying for a stranger enables us to connect to the great mystery of life and the human family.

At my church we have given away hundreds of shawls to unknown friends over the years. We have learned that, like the story of the Good Samaritan in Luke 10: 30–37, knitting for our neighbor allows us to care for people regardless of their race, religion, or nationality. We are all God's children. People who receive a shawl feel and appreciate our prayers; these prayers touch the lives of others and are sometimes transformative. Some years ago a nurse asked me for a shawl for a young man in his thirties. He was paralyzed, dying, and angry about both. Even though we did not know this man, we learned from the nurse that the shawl we had given him brought him comfort. His caretakers were amazed at the change in him. Wrapped in his shawl, he died in peace.

Part of the journey of prayer and faith is to recognize that we may never know how our love and care will touch or change another person's life. Instead, we are invited to offer others our compassion and let whatever needs to happen, happen. There is an old saying: "Our hands are God's hands." Through the shawl-knitting ministry we can learn to trust the truth that God works through us when we care for friends and strangers alike.

Finally, there are times when we begin to knit a shawl that we think will go to a stranger, only to discover part way through that we know exactly whom we

Peace I leave with you, my peace I give to you; not as the world gives do I give to you. Let not your hearts be troubled, neither let them be afraid.

JOHN 14:27 RSV

The Lord is near to the brokenhearted and saves the crushed in spirit.

PSALM 34:18 RSV

*In all
circumstances
give thanks,
for this is the will
of God for you.*

1 Thessalonians 5:18

are knitting for. These are wonderful moments of grace, epiphanies, revelations. There is a sense of delight and joy when we suddenly envision a specific person wrapped in the shawl. While on vacation a while ago I stopped by a yarn shop (I tend to hunt them down wherever I am) and bought some ribbon yarn for a shawl. The unusual mixture of blues, greens, and black looked like it would make an interesting shawl. Because of the elastic texture, the yarn was difficult to knit, and I had to start it a few times in order to get the correct number of stitches and needle size. I had no idea who would receive the shawl until I was sitting at a concert at my youngest daughter's music camp; suddenly I knew it would be for her violin teacher. It would be a thank-you shawl for all she had given my daughter and all her other students over the years, a shawl of gratitude for the gift of music she has given to my family and many other people.

Once I knew for whom I was knitting, I didn't mind that the yarn was difficult to knit. Instead, I was filled with thanks for this woman and grateful I could knit a shawl for her. Whether or not we know the people who will receive them, knitting shawls deepens our understanding of God's presence in our lives and also invites us to care for our neighbors with thanksgiving and joy.

CHAPTER 5
SELECTING YARN

Susan S. Izard

Yarn stores are my sanctuary.[18]

—LISA AVERYHART

*S*electing the yarn for a shawl can be a fun, creative, and inspiring process. Picking the weight of yarn to use is the first step. The yarn you choose will depend upon where the shawl recipient lives and the reason why you are knitting the shawl. Generally, heavier yarns work for people who live in colder climates; lighter yarns work for those in warmer climates. People who are sick and feeling weak have told us that they appreciate lighter weight shawls. They also appreciate having shawls knit with yarn that can be easily washed. It is important to be sensitive to the circumstances and preferences of the people for whom you are knitting.

If this is your first shawl, I suggest that you use yarn that is soft, fairly thick, lightweight, and has some texture to it. When you knit with this type of yarn on size 13 (9 in countries that use metric measurements) needles, the shawl has an airy, open look. The reason that I look for yarn with texture is because thinner, smoother yarns create shawls with gaping holes when knit with this size needle. Shawls knit with thicker, textured yarn will be warm but not heavy, comfortable but not overbearing. The K3, P3 pattern will be very noticeable when you use smoother yarns; this type of yarn usually requires smaller needles (to avoid the gaping holes) and more stitches to achieve the correct size.

Choosing the color of your yarn is the second step. When you are knitting a shawl with someone in mind, consider which color the person receiving the shawl might look best in or like the most. If you are knitting a shawl that will be donated or given to someone you do not know, choose a color that you like or that captures your eye. The process of knitting a shawl will be more interesting and satisfying if you are knitting with a color and yarn that you enjoy looking at and touching.

Some yarns are variegated, some create stripes, some are heathery, and some are a solid color. It's fun to see all the different shawls that emerge from one pattern and many different types of yarn. The people in our knitting circle are always commenting on the beauty and the colors of the shawls that each person is knitting. I often hear women say, "I want to knit that color next. What is its name?"

While you may pick a yarn for its color, some yarn manufacturers name their yarns. Susan chose to knit in *Navajo*[19] for a woman who had worked on an Indian reservation for several years. Another time, she chose *Prairie* because the woman for whom she knit the shawl had lived in Kansas her entire life, as had her parents and grandparents. Susan is in the process of knitting *Pacifica* for her daughter, whose dream was to travel to the Pacific Ocean after she finished college. There seem to be as many ways to choose yarn as there are colors and textures.

Now Israel loved Joseph more than all his children, because he was the son of his old age; and he made him a coat of many colors.

GENESIS 37:3 KJV

One woman in our circle who has knit over fifty shawls for the ministry uses up her extra yarn by knitting "Joseph shawls." She takes a variety of left-over colors and makes a shawl of many colors, similar to Joseph's Coat of Many Colors (Genesis 37:3). She often uses different colors of yarn for the fringe of her regular shawls to make them unique and to use up extra yarn. Another woman didn't like the idea of knitting a shawl with only one type of yarn, so she added an interesting mohair yarn in a variety of places throughout the garment. The result was magnificent. So, while your first few shawls may follow the exact pattern and yarn recommended in this book, allow yourself to be more creative as your confidence grows; there is no right or wrong in this ministry.

When I am ready to start a new shawl, I go to a yarn store with an open mind and heart. I like to walk around the store and wait until a certain yarn inspires me. Sometimes I know what color I am looking for. Sometimes I know for whom I am knitting. Sometimes I am there for other reasons but stumble across a perfect yarn for a shawl and take it home with me. Let the Spirit be your guide when shopping for yarn, and follow your instincts in choosing colors and types of yarn.

Last year my oldest daughter was graduating from high school. I wanted to make her a special shawl that she would have for many years. I knew I wanted to use yarn that looked and felt festive, and I wanted the shawl to be blue, but I did not know what hue(s) of blue. I ended up buying a wool bouclé that had a variety of blue tones that resembled the ocean and was fairly thin. Once completed, the shawl was lightweight and warm; the bumps of the bouclé gave it the texture I wanted.

Sometimes I have picked yarn that does not work with size 13 (9) needles. It is fine to experiment and figure out what size needles are needed. I am currently knitting a shawl with size 17 (12) needles. The thickness and texture of the yarn I am using requires the use of the enormous needles. If you choose a

Take me to a yarn store anytime. . . . Yarn stores are my sanctuary, a place where my creativity flows unchecked and I leave my troubles outside the front door.[20]

LISA C. AVERYHART

needle other than size 13 (9), you will need to adjust the number of stitches you cast on: add more stitches with smaller needles and decrease the number for larger ones. After knitting a swatch of the yarn, I decided to cast on 51 stitches for this shawl. The shawl has knit up quickly; its whimsical color of red with pink flecks and soft texture of wool, polyamide, acrylic, and polyester has created a spectacular shawl, just right for the artist who is to receive it.

Another way of finding unique and different yarn is to explore yarn shops when you are on vacation. Last summer I stopped by a yarn shop in Vermont where all the yarn is made on site. I bought some lovely fine white wool that I thought would knit into a light, lacy shawl. When I started knitting, however, I didn't like the way it looked. The yarn didn't have enough texture to work well with the size 13 (9) needles. Instead of looking light and airy, it looked loose and sloppy. While in New Hampshire I found some very fine mohair in exactly the same color white as the wool from the store in Vermont. When I added the mohair to the wool and knit the two strands together, the mohair created the texture I needed to make the shawl work. The result was a lovely winter white shawl that was light and lacy to look at, but very warm. Fortunately, it was given to a woman in Maine who could appreciate its warmth on the long winter nights.

Sometimes an interest in the type of yarn will inspire you to start knitting a shawl even when you do not have a particular person in mind. One day I came across a glorious skein of yarn made with mohair, viscose, metal, acrylic, and nylon. The color was a mixture of lavender, green, and yellow hues with gold metallic thread woven into it. I didn't know who would receive this shawl, but I knew I wanted to make a shawl from this yarn. While knitting on the shawl at a meeting, a friend was as taken by the yarn as I was. During the meeting she announced that she was to be ordained that year. It occurred to me that the shawl was for her—an ordination shawl. The colors and texture of the yarn were perfect for this type of celebration. When I bought the yarn I had a hunch that a shawl made from this yarn would find just the right home. It did.

The creative experience of knitting a shawl can even inspire you to make your own yarn. Early in the ministry I received a letter from a cloistered nun in England who wanted to introduce the shawl-knitting ministry to her community. She explained that each sister prayed in her own cell in the morning. Many of them were interested in knitting shawls while they were praying. They wanted more information on the ministry. I sent her a packet of yarn, needles, and directions so she could make a shawl and see if there was any yarn in England that would be comparable to what I sent her. She wrote back saying that they had located a wholesale yarn dealer in northern England and were trying out a variety of different yarns to see how they worked. She was particularly excited about some natural mohair yarn that she dyed with heather and rhubarb from the convent's garden. The heather made a beautiful pink/brown, the rhubarb root a deep gold. Knitting the shawls with home-dyed yarn made the shawls all the more meaningful for the convent.

Selecting yarn for a shawl can be a fun, creative, and inspiring process. It can also be an experience of prayer and entering into Mystery. By holding the recipient of the shawl, known or unknown, in your thoughts and prayers as you choose your yarn, you enter into a sacred journey of knitting with the Holy One. Your hands become a tangible instrument of God's love. God's creative spirit encourages you to personalize the shawls through the color and texture of the yarn. As you pay attention to your instinctive, intuitive responses to the yarn, you connect with this creative spirit. By honoring this process of selecting yarn, you begin the journey of creating a shawl that will wrap one of God's beloved children in warmth and compassion.

There is an ecstasy in the act of creation that matches the intensity of religious rapture; both partake of divinity and are gifts granted by the Great Creative Spirit.[21]

SUSAN GORDON LYDON

CHAPTER 6
BASIC INSTRUCTIONS

Susan S. Jorgensen

For all these mysteries, I thank you:
for the wonder of myself, for the wonder of your works.

—Psalm 139:14 JB

To begin at the beginning is to say that the idea of knitting shawls for others and the original shawl pattern were developed by Janet Bristow and Victoria Cole-Galo. Susan and I are indebted to the gift they have given to us and to all who engage in this ministry, and we honor the creativity of the Spirit as it is expressed through them in this particular way.

The original shawl is based on a K3, P3 pattern. Before getting into the basic instructions for this shawl, I would like to explore the significance of the K3, P3 pattern. Deciding to make a shawl in this pattern was not a random event for Vicky. In her story about the shawl-knitting ministry, which appears on page 109, Vicky said that she didn't want to create "just any shawl. . . . The pattern of knitting in threes . . . came to me in prayer." The website that Janet and Vicky (www.shawlministry.com) maintain describes in detail the significance of this pattern of threes. Let me say a few things here.

The pattern of threes can be found in every religion and society. Human existence has three stages: birth, life, and death. Time has three divisions: past, present, and future. The panorama of colors is based on three primary colors. Human "being" has three parts: body, mind, and spirit. The virtues frequently mentioned together are faith, hope, and love (1 Corinthians 12). The rhythm of the waltz is 1–2–3, 1–2–3, 1–2–3. The ability to compromise—to take two seemingly different (and oftentimes hotly disputed) points of view and create a third possibility—is another way the pattern of threes plays out in our world: not this or that, but this (w)holy other thing. Upon this ability to see the third, peace springs forth if we have eyes to see it.

Knitting Instructions

These instructions assume you know how to knit already.
Note: The second set of numbers is for our friends who use the metric system.

1. *Decide what size needle you will use.* Size 11 (8) needles create a slightly denser shawl and the K3, P3 pattern will be more noticeable. Conversely, size 13 (9) needles create a slightly looser, less definable pattern. Approximate finished sizes, not counting fringe, are 26" x 60" on size 11 needles (66 cm x 152 cm on 8) and 30" x 64" on 13 needles (76 cm x 162 cm on 9). You may use smaller or larger needles as well, depending on the yarn that you have chosen; knit up a sample and do the math so that your shawl is the size you desire. The smaller the needle, the more stitches you will need; the larger the needle, the fewer.

Buddhists say that enlightenment may be achieved through the repetition of sutra, or prayer. Pattern also is formed by repetition; its beauty deepens and grows each time it is repeated.[22]

Susan Gordon Lydon

2. *Select your yarn.* You might pick a yarn for its color, for its name, or for its texture as described in the previous chapter. A standard shawl requires three skeins of yarn that are six ounces (170 g) net weight and 185 yards (166.5 m) each.

3. *Cast on.* Cast on 57 stitches for size 13 (9) needles, 63 for size 11 (8). The pattern is K3, P3 every row. This means that you will always begin each row with K3 and end each row with K3. The pattern is a modified seed or moss stitch. Any odd multiple of three will work for your shawl, depending on how wide you want to make it: 57, 63, 69, 75, 81, and so on. Follow this pattern until you achieve the desired length. You may also decide to knit every row, which is called a garter stitch. **Before you begin the third skein, make your fringe.**

   An alternative for men: If the gift is going to a man, making a lap blanket may be a good alternative to the shawl. In this case, cast on 87 stitches (size 13 (9)). This gives you a blanket approximately 45" (114 cm) wide. Use four skeins for this project. Rather than fringe, consider creating a selvage edge by crocheting a single crochet around the entire blanket. If you decide to do this, make sure you reserve yarn for that.

4. *Attaching the next skein or ball.* An alternative to tying a knot and then weaving the ends of the two strands of yarn into the shawl when you are all done is to weave the new end into the old with a darning needle. This eliminates knots and having to weave in all those ends (a tedious process at best). Clip the ends of both pieces of yarn. Thread the needle with the end of the new skein. Beginning at the end of the skein you are finishing, hold the end taut and insert the needle. Take tiny stitches in a slightly spiral fashion, maintaining firm and even tension. When you have woven

through about three inches, pull gently to test the yarn. It should hold. If it slips or pulls out, continue to take tiny stitches through the old yarn or start again. The result should be a joined piece of yarn that is smooth and slightly thicker than a single strand; it disappears easily into the fabric of the shawl. Take care as you knit the joint. Once you have knit the joint into the shawl, you can clip the ends that have frayed in the knitting process (generally quite short). This process works with thin or thick, smooth or nubby yarn.

5. *Selvages.* You may want to create a selvage edge for your shawl. This creates a smoother finish for the sides of your shawl. At the beginning of each row, slip the first stitch purlwise; the yarn will be in front of your work. Carry the yarn to the back, K2, and continue with the pattern to the end of the row.

6. *Make fringe.* The length of the fringe is an individual decision. It can be long or short. You can put a piece of fringe through every stitch, or you can skip several stitches. Some people tie or sew beads to fringe, especially if the shawl is for a child. Whatever your preference, here is what you do:

   Decide how long you want the fringe. Because the fringe is doubled when you fasten it to the shawl, you must cut the fringe twice the desired length: for 6" (15 cm) fringe, each piece must be 12" (30 cm) long; for 12" (30 cm) fringe, cut pieces 24" (60 cm); and so on. A stiff piece of cardboard cut to the finished length of the fringe helps with this process. Wrap the yarn around the cardboard as many times as you want pieces of fringe, and cut only one end.

   For standard fringe, cut 57 (63) lengths for each end of the shawl, or 114 (126) total. Reserve fringe until you have finished knitting the shawl.

I tie each bundle with a slipknot to keep from losing them and getting them tangled, and put them in a sealed plastic bag for safekeeping.

7. *Finish the shawl.* Attach the inside end of the third skein of yarn to your shawl and continue knitting until all the yarn is used up, or until you have achieved the desired length.

8. *Attach the fringe.* Double the yarn and, using a small crochet hook, pull the loop through the stitch; insert the ends of the fringe through the loop and pull tight, creating a knot.

    Victoria A. Cole-Galo creates fringe with a tassel effect. She uses two strands of yarn that she doubles and then inserts in every third stitch where the trough or ridge is created when you change from knit to purl and vice versa. This creates fringe that is eight strands thick, spaced every third stitch. You may find the details of this process on her website.

9. *Knot the ends of the fringe.* Some people knot the ends of each strand to keep the fringe from fraying. This is an individual decision. Some people would rather leave it alone. I prefer to knot the ends when I am using any yarn that frays easily.

10. *Give away your shawl.* If you are making the shawl for a particular person, you may want to include the history of the shawl-knitting ministry and a prayer. Many people wrap the shawl in tissue and tie it with a leftover piece of yarn. See Chapter 10, "Giving Away a Shawl," page 81 for more on this.

A modified version of this pattern appears on page 145. Please feel free to copy it as the need arises.

Crochet Instructions

Use a size M hook. Chain 54 stitches or desired width of shawl. Chain 1, turn, single crochet in each of the stitches to end. Chain 3 and turn. Double crochet in top of each single crochet. Repeat this row two more times. Chain 1 and do 1 row of single crochet to end. Chain 3 and turn. Do 3 rows of double crochet. Repeat pattern to end (1 row single, 3 rows double) End with 1 row of single. Finish with fringe. *This pattern was developed by Rita Glod and is used with permission.*

Crocheting typically uses more yarn than knitting, so consider buying four skeins or making your shawl narrower or shorter. If you purchase four skeins, you will probably have yarn left over (for your Joseph shawl).

Knitters around the world are developing other shawl patterns. We praise their ingenuity and creativity. At the same time, people frequently share stories with us about wearing a shawl knit in the K3, P3 pattern in a public place; someone will invariably exclaim, "That's one of those shawls, isn't it? Tell me where you got it!" There will always be tension between conformity that brings with it the delight of immediate recognition and a sense of solidarity, and the creativity that makes individual expression possible. It would be a sad and dull world indeed if we all wore orange shirts and khaki pants. May your choices for knitting shawls be guided by the urgings and groanings of the Spirit.

. . . the Spirit itself intercedes with inexpressible groanings.

Romans 8:26

PART THREE

KNITTING

CHAPTER 7
KNITTING "ALONE"

Susan S. Izard

The important thing is not so much what you knit as
what happens to you while you knit it. Where the interior
journey takes you. What you find there. How you are
transformed when you come back home.[23]

— SUSAN GORDON LYDON

Knitting a shawl alone can be a relaxing, peaceful activity. Many of us lead hectic lives filled with multiple responsibilities. Finding time to sit and knit can be wonderfully rejuvenating and calming. Knitting allows us to sit and relax our bodies as well as our minds. Once the K3, P3 pattern is established, you don't need to think very hard about knitting a shawl. You can allow yourself to surrender to the repetitive movement of your hands and relax into the flow of knitting. Having a shawl to knit can also be a way to occupy our hands as we wait in the doctor's office, sit through meetings, or wait for children to finish a lesson or activity. Over the past few years, I have sat through hours of my younger daughter's violin lessons knitting shawls. I have come to look forward to her lesson, not just because I love listening to her play, but also because I love to knit for an hour without any interruptions.

Knitting alone can be more than a peaceful, rejuvenating activity, however. It can be a time for contemplative prayer and a window into Mystery. In her book, *The Practice of Prayer*, Margaret Guenther reminds us that the desert father, Abba Arsenius, gives three commands about prayer: "'*Fuge!*' Flee! Remove yourself physically to a quiet place, away from distractions good and bad. '*Tace!*' Be silent! Stop talking. '*Quiesce!*' Be inwardly still."[25] These instructions are also good guidelines for practicing knitting as contemplative prayer.

Fuge, or "flee," is the first step in knitting alone. Find a place in your home where you can be alone to knit. For those of you who live alone or have long periods of time when you are alone in your homes, this is easy. A favorite chair in the den or living room can be a perfect place for quiet knitting. For others who still have children at home, pets who adore you and want to be with you at every moment, or partners or spouses who work at home, this can be more of a challenge. It might require some ingenuity to find a place to knit and pray contemplatively. Sometimes it means creating a prayer corner in your bedroom, basement, or attic where you can close the door and set yourself apart. One woman told me she took an old junk closet and turned it into her prayer room. She cleaned everything out, repainted it, and placed a small chair and lamp in the closet along with devotional objects that she loved. She was delighted to have created her own prayer space. As you search for a prayer space, trust your inner desire to find a place to knit contemplatively and be creative until you find it, even if it means sitting in your car or finding a park bench where people won't interrupt you.

Needles . . . click the click of comfort, of a crackling fire, of a rocking chair by a cradle, the click of warmth and security.[24]

SHULAMITH OPPENHEIM

Tace, or "be silent," is the second step in knitting alone. "Be still, and know that I am God," writes the Psalmist in Psalm 46:10 (RSV). Contemplative prayer requires silence, but that's often hard to find. In our postmodern era, our lives are filled with noise. But being quiet means leaving noise and interruptions behind. Excuse yourself from family members for a half an hour or so, and turn off the television, radio, computer and telephone. Even harder, being quiet and contemplative means resolving within yourself that you won't answer the door bell or respond to any kind of interruption during this time of prayerful knitting. As best as possible, create an atmosphere of silence in order to be present to God in contemplative prayer.

Becoming inwardly still, *quiesce*, is the third step in knitting alone. Once you have settled in your quiet space with your knitting and separated yourself from the various distractions, become inwardly still and wait into the silence for the presence of God. Sometimes it helps to begin with intercessory prayer for the person for whom you're knitting. You might also choose to begin with a favorite prayer or hymn to help get settled into the quiet and be still. Knitting in silence gives God an opportunity to be with you, nurture you, guide you, and heal you. As you knit in silence, you wait for the Mystery of God to unfold within you.

Unfortunately, becoming inwardly silent is often difficult. Even though you create a quiet environment, you might find that your inner world is noisy and cluttered. Real silence can seem almost impossible. All kinds of inner thoughts can interrupt the silence. The schedule for the day can pop into your head. All of a sudden, you find yourself making mental notes about the things you need to do—you must not forget apples at the grocery store or to call the person you forgot about yesterday. Conversations you want to have, vacations you want to

It is in silence that we can truly acknowledge who we are and gradually claim ourselves as a gift from God.[26]

HENRI J. M. NOUWEN

go on, or old memories that creep in can all interrupt your attempt to find inner silence and quiet time to listen for God.

Father Thomas Keating, the champion of centering prayer, suggests that when you find yourself preoccupied with your thoughts rather than resting in inner silence, you let go of those thoughts and return to your original desire for inner quiet. In centering prayer, a prayer word is used to bring you back to inner stillness. With contemplative knitting, K3, P3 can be a way to return to inner quiet. By refocusing on the rhythm of the knitting, you can return to inner stillness and God's presence. The flow of your hands can be the grounding point for this contemplative prayer.

Letting go of inner busyness and sinking into the silence of God is one way you can experience God's presence. Your knitting and your very being will be blessed.

Contemplation is a deep resonance in the inmost center of our spirit in which our very life loses its separate voice and re-sounds with the majesty and the mercy of the Hidden and Living One.[27]

THOMAS MERTON

A Shawl Prayer

This shawl has been knit for:

_____

By: _____

Let us pray this blessing:

_____

_____

_____

_____

On this date, _____

and around our gathered circle, this
shawl has passed through our praying
hands and been blessed by our loving
hearts.

CHAPTER 8
KNITTING WITH OTHERS

Susan S. Jorgensen

Community is like a large mosaic . . . a fellowship of little
people who together make God visible in the world.[28]

—HENRI J. M. NOUWEN

$\mathcal{M}$any of us knit alone; it can be a solitary art, much like writing or painting or practicing music. I do most of my shawl knitting in waiting rooms,
between direction appointments, while watching television, sitting by the fire
on a cold winter night or in a patch of sun on a summer afternoon, and in the
car (when someone else is driving!). That said, the art of knitting is most often
passed on in community. The experience of two people, side by side, heads
bent in intense concentration, one holding the yarn and teaching, the other
listening and watching, is perhaps *the* most common way knitting is taught—
in a community of two. And while we may read books about knitting and our

*In our career-
driven age,
you can choose to
define yourself as a
knitter rather than
as a lawyer, a
physical therapist, a
bank teller. You are
the recipient and
conduit of an old
and precious craft.
If you teach
someone else to
knit, you open this
world to her.*[29]

LISA R. MYERS

ability to follow patterns may sharpen and improve, there are subtleties in knitting that are difficult to describe and much easier to demonstrate face-to-face.

Even if your time knitting with another is not spent teaching or learning, something significant happens when you gather to share your mutual love and passion for the craft. This social aspect of knitting is important. My guess is that if you are part of a shawl-knitting circle, it has become a priority in your life. You may cross other things off your calendar in an effort to simplify your life, but you probably stop short of canceling your time with your knitting circle. Some circles gather weekly. Ours gathers monthly. Knitting circles are fun and funny, full of laughter and great stories; they are reverent, humble, and humbling as shawl after shawl emerges from its own invisible womb to be passed around the circle and blessed by each knitter's hands. Over and over the circle becomes and extends far beyond its individual parts. If one knitter doesn't know how to fix a particular gaffe, chances are another one does. Two heads (almost) always work better than one.

The first night of my first knitting circle was nearly a disaster. I had blithely advertised that no knitting experience was needed, that "we" would teach you. In retrospect, I had not thought through who this invisible "we" was, since I was the sole organizer. Several people who came needed to be reminded how to cast on or how to purl. One or two said, "I have never knit before." I was smiling (on the outside) as we went around the circle, introducing ourselves. But looking at the expectant faces around me, I was desperately trying to figure out how "I" was going to do this.

Thankfully, many seasoned knitters were there who were ready to pitch in. The lonely "I" became a willing "we." To my surprise (and great relief), by the end of the night each person had at least a row or two on her needles. "Formal" prayer went the way of a forgotten art that first chaotic night, even as the Spirit of all that is made a grand entrance in the form of a community working together and supporting itself. Since then, I have pondered the wisdom of advertising that no experience was necessary. The desire to open the shawl-knitting ministry to both the novice as well as the seasoned knitter was an honorable one. But I now advise anyone starting a group to ask people as they sign up whether or not they can knit. And plan accordingly.

Starting Your Own Knitting Circle

What follows is a simple format for a knitting circle. Having no desire to become a self-appointed guru, I offer it humbly, trusting that there is no single way to organize a knitting circle. I invite each of you who facilitate a group to trust your own intuition, instincts, and experience, and invite the Spirit to be with you as your group grows and changes. A good way to begin a new group is to invite all those who come to talk about how they learned to knit. More than an icebreaker, these stories create and reveal a common language and bond that feels pure and devoid of pretense.

Our group gathers for an hour and a half each month; we begin with opening prayer. As the facilitator I am responsible for leading this prayer, and I have been using the prayers found at the end of this chapter. You may want to invite various people to volunteer for that task; it will depend entirely on the makeup of your group and your own leadership style.

Quite often, we find ourselves rushing through prayers. It might be helpful, especially in the beginning stages of your knitting circle, to invite the members of your circle, as they pray, to savor the sound and the feel of each word and phrase in their mouths and on their tongues. Praying involves mind and heart, body and soul. The effort that is required is not as much about taking time as it is about cultivating and nurturing the right attitude. The time we

*Ever present
in your midst,
I will be your God,
and you will be
my people.*

LEVITICUS 26:12

spend paying attention and being intentional is not long; the effect is noticeable and well worth the effort. The prayers we offer at the end of this chapter can be prayed in unison, or you can move around your circle line by line or paragraph by paragraph where the prayer lends itself to that.

After prayer, we knit and listen to stories about the shawls that have been given away since we last met. We share notes, letters, and cards from those who have received shawls. Anyone who needs help with some part of his or her shawl speaks up, and someone is always willing to offer assistance or advice. We spend about one hour actually knitting.

Then we ask if there are any shawls that will be given away before we next meet. Each person who has or will be completing a shawl says a bit about the person for whom they have knit the shawl and why. Sometimes, we don't know the name of the person who will receive the shawl, though we often know who will be distributing them and for what general purpose. One of our members, for example, is knitting shawls for use by people who are undergoing radiation at a local hospital.

Once we have heard about the shawls to be given away, we bless them. We often bless as many as six or eight around our circle on any given night. We pray for specific intentions when we know why a person is receiving a shawl; when we don't know, we pray healing, light, hope, and comfort into the shawl. At times, we've found it difficult to remember which shawl is for whom and what the recipient's need might be. So now knitters include a card for each of the shawls, providing as much or as little information as they feel comfortable with. Each card is a quarter of an 8½" x 11" (22 cm x 28 cm) sheet of paper, and it is printed on card stock. The card is punched; a ribbon is inserted through the hole and then attached carefully to the shawl with a safety pin. This is the information from our card:

Through the lens of story we see the mystery of ourselves more clearly.[30]

SUE MONK KIDD

This shawl has been knit for:

_____ _____

(Name of person, if known, is written here)

By: _____

_____

(Name of knitter)

Let us pray this blessing for her or him:

_____ _____

_____ _____

_____ _____

                (on these lines the knitter can write
                a single word or an entire prayer)

On this date, _____ _____ _____

               (the date the shawl was blessed)

and around our gathered circle, this shawl has passed through our praying hands and been blessed by our loving hearts.

A Shawl Prayer

This shawl has been knit for:
Molly
By: *Susie*

Let us pray this blessing:
Be well . . .
Be warm . . .
Be loved . . .
Be comforted . . .

On this date, *11 · March · 05*
and around our gathered circle, this shawl has passed through our praying hands and been blessed by our loving hearts.

    Some people share only the briefest of stories and give just a little information. Others have been known to write a full prayer or blessing (in very tiny writing!). Once we have filled out the cards and attached them to the shawls we are blessing, we enter into silence and pass each shawl from person to person. We tenderly hold each shawl as we bless it and pray over it. The sound of the silence is palpable, reverent, and beautiful to behold. It is the sound of the prayer of our hearts, the sound of our hope and deepest longing for others. It is the sound of our blessings being gathered and ascending to the waiting ear of Mystery.

Some groups will prefer praying a written blessing for each shawl or praying aloud spontaneously, trusting the movement of the Spirit. Either way is fine. One blessing prayer for the shawl can be found on page 68 of this chapter.

Surprisingly, blessing the shawls, even if there are six or eight, doesn't take long. Some of us leave the cards attached to our shawls when we give them away; some of us remove them. There is no set process or rule of thumb. Honor what is comfortable for you and the person who is receiving the shawl. We conclude our evening with a prayer. Several samples can be found at the end of this chapter.

I am a record keeper by nature; some people refer to my type as "pack rats." I have a stack of journals that attest to my addiction. I keep old appointment books, checkbook records, and, even worse, canceled checks. I say this as a preface to the suggestion that you might want to keep a record for your knitting circle. We keep a list of who comes each night (a simple sign-in sheet with the date at the top), a list of the shawls that we give away, and the prayer intention for that shawl.

Eventually, we will organize all of this in a three-ring binder as a way to honor and remember the work of our hands and the prayer of our hearts. You may want to include photos of completed shawls and circle members. These efforts—small in nature, lasting in effect—are among the building blocks of your community. They communicate love and care, and let the members of your circle know that who they are and what they do here is important.

We have no formal rules or guidelines. Our gathering is simple, informal, and straight from the heart. We know that we are not a therapy or support group; we are not about exploring deep or sensitive issues that require rules of confidentiality. We are here to knit; we are here because each of us, in our own unique way, has encountered the Mystery into which our craft inevitably leads us. We laugh a lot, we share what we know, we learn from one another. A simple love between people who love the same art is awakening and taking root, filling our circle with joy and delight.

Your circle may be more comfortable with a few clear rules. If so, may these four suggestions guide your process:

1. As you craft these rules, spend time together in prayer;

2. Make sure that whatever guidelines you set forth come from a place of conversation with your God;

3. Revisit them periodically to see if they still remain true and represent the spirit of your circle;

4. Hold them always with a gentle and compassionate heart.

There is another way to create community that doesn't necessarily involve the creation of a knitting circle, and that is the experience of having more than one person knit on a shawl for someone. The shawl may be passed from person to person around a knitting circle so that each person can knit a row or two. Or, a shawl may pass from home to home, with each knitter adding a previously agreed upon number of rows and then passing it to the next person. In this way, the shawl recipient has been given a tangible expression of a community's heart and the work of its hands. I had the privilege of doing this with a shawl that one of my directees was knitting for her daughter, whom I have come to know and love. Knitting three rows of her shawl gave me the opportunity to pass a small piece of myself along with my prayer for her; I was deeply moved.

We offer several gathering prayers and blessings suitable for opening your circle, and one for closing. Pick and choose as the Spirit moves you. As with all of the prayers in this book, they are yours to use within your knitting circles.

A Prayer of Gathering

Susan S. Izard

Gracious God,
God of Life, God of Love, God of Compassion,

We give you thanks for your abiding presence and our shared joy that you are our God and we are your people. We give you thanks for the gathering of our knitting circle. We give you thanks for the shawls we create. We give you thanks for each other and all those for whom we knit.

Bless, O God, our time together. Bless our hearts that they might be filled with your Spirit. Bless our hands that they might be touched by your creative power. Bless our knitting that the shawls may be filled with your love.

Gather us, Holy One, in your embracing arms. Fill us with your tender mercy. Nurture us with your compassionate presence. Breathe in us the gift of your grace so that our hearts may be your Heart, our hands may be your Hands, and our work may be your Work, now and forever more.

Amen.

Opening Prayer

SUSAN S. JORGENSEN

Leader of Prayer: Let us begin with a moment of silence so that we might notice how we are right now (*pause as we settle in*); so that we might notice who we are right now (*pause and invite each person to notice each person in the circle*).

As we gather for this time of knitting together in community,

> May a Spirit of comfort ease the burdens of our day;
>
> May a Spirit of peace descend upon us;
>
> May a Spirit of love open our listening hearts;
>
> May a Spirit of wisdom guide the work of our hands.
>
> May we be filled by a Spirit of gratitude for this time of communion;
>
> May we be filled by a Spirit of appreciation for all who are here and for those who are absent.
>
> *Amen.*

Prayer of Blessing

CATHLEEN MURTHA, DW

Leader of Prayer: As we prepare to share our prayer, our stories, the work of our hearts and hands, we pray for God's blessing on our endeavors:

A *blessing* to my mind (*pause for a moment*) to be free to
enter this time of contemplative activity . . .

A blessing to my hands (*pause for a moment*) to be the source of
creating something of beauty and love . . .

A blessing to my soul (*pause for a moment*) to be open to the
promptings of prayer and reflection . . .

A blessing to my yarn (*pause for a moment*) to be shaped into patterns of loving and caring . . .

A blessing to my needles (*pause for a moment*) to be the holders of
stitches as they become a whole garment . . .

A blessing to my knitting (*pause for a moment*) to be a work of
heart and hands, body and spirit . . .

A blessing on the one who passed this ancient art to me . . .

A blessing on the one who will receive the fruit of my prayer and
my knitting . . .

May this shawl be welcomed in the spirit in which it was knit . . .

May we become one with the One who knitted each of us in our
mother's womb.

We join our blessing, our prayer, and our knitting with women
and men all over the earth in this common effort to bring
healing and wholeness, comfort and celebration.

Amen.

Begin to Knit

KENT IRA GROFF

Begin to knit, and God will show you the pattern
and give you the yarn.

—ADAPTED FROM A GERMAN PROVERB

May I begin, O God, and merely begin
again to knit essential habits of the heart
in this my life . . . in this our community . . .
May I begin by listening . . . yes listening
to the rapid beating within my heart . . .
to the slow rhythm of my breathing . . .
to the clatter and pain of the world . . .
to a still small voice that says, Peace:
Be still . . . and know that I am God . . .
Be still . . . and know that I am God . . .
Be still . . . and know that I am God . . .

Let me be open to surprise as you show

the unique pattern for my life to grow

in solitude . . . and in solidarity with all . . .

[*Name persons . . . institutions . . . places . . .*]

Knit your Love throughout my life,

till I wear it like a well-worn garment,

suited well for my unique frame within,

suited to changes of time and place without,

keeping me secure in your changeless Love

and always facing toward the world with hope;

for the sake of your Name and for the sake of the world.

AMEN—MAY IT BE SO.

Prayer of Our Hands

SUSAN S. JORGENSEN

*B*ecause our hands are so integral to this shawl-knitting ministry, you may, at some point, for variety, want to begin your circle with a meditation that focuses on the gift of our hands. Again, remind the group that this prayer need not be rushed and that each person will benefit from slowing down in order to notice God's presence, in order to create the opening into which Mystery and grace will enter.

Once the circle has gathered and settled, introduce the prayer by mentioning how important our hands are to this shawl-knitting ministry. Ask everyone to take a few deep breaths to guide them into the quiet space within. Invite everyone to rest their hands in their laps, palms down. Ask them to look at their hands, to gaze, to notice them as if they were seeing them for the first time. *Pause for at least ten seconds to allow each person to do this in silence.*

Invite each person to shift their gaze to the hands of the people in the circle, noticing simply and with intention. Once you, as the leader of the prayer, have completed the circle, invite each person to turn their palms up and notice their hands in this position. Again, this is done in silence. After about ten seconds or so, ask each person to gaze at the palms of the other people in the circle. Once you are finished, call everyone to prayer:

Let us pray,

Loving God, we give you thanks for the gift of our hands. Give us the grace to see our hands as you see them, as instruments of grace and life. May the knitting of our hands be the knitting of your heart. Use our hands, O God, to carry out your works of mercy and love. May the shawls our hands create bring blessing to those they wrap in love and healing to those upon whom they rest.
Amen.

Prayer of Blessing
for a Completed Shawl

JANET BRISTOW

May God's grace be upon this shawl . . .
warming, comforting,
enfolding and embracing.

May this mantle be a safe haven . . .
a sacred place of security and well-being . . .
sustaining and embracing in good times as well as difficult ones.

May the one who receives this shawl
be cradled in hope, kept in joy, graced with peace,
and wrapped in love.

Blessed Be!

Closing Prayer and Blessing

Susan S. Jorgensen

Before beginning this prayer, invite your group to finish their row, and to rest their shawls and needles in their laps.

Leader of Prayer:	Let us bring our gathering to a close and gather the work of our hands with intention and purpose.
All:	Loving God, as we gaze upon this holy work within our circle, may our hearts be filled by what we see. May we behold you in the steady flow of yarn to needle, in the gentle weight of shawls growing long, in the many colors and textures here before us.
Leader of Prayer:	Let us give voice to the gratitude and love that rest within our hearts.
All:	Generous God, we thank you for bringing us together in this circle. We thank you for the gift of knitting and the gift of praying. We thank you for those who have passed on this ancient art to us. We thank you for those who created the yarn, those who brought it to market, those who stocked the shelves. We are blessed by the lives of the many people who make our knitting possible.

Leader of Prayer:	Let us pray for those who will receive these shawls.
All:	Compassionate God, we ask you to bless all the people for whom these shawls are being knit. May these shawls be a reminder of your presence in their lives. May these shawls bring them love and light, hope and joy.
Leader of Prayer:	Let us pray for a safe trip home.
All:	O God, you who watch over us by day and by night, keep us safe from harm. Guide us to our homes with care and love. Be a bright light in our darkness. Grant us rest in the midst of our hectic lives. Bless us; bless those we love; bless especially those in pain and loneliness.

Amen.

Betsy...

be with you now and always:

and calm

comfort and

peace,

Deep river of love and

Given to my dear friend on 21. February. 2003.
Started and Finished January, 2003.

HOMESPUN®

Color No.	Art. No. 790	Lot No.
365 PAGODA	1207	99365418

0 23032 79365 8

CHAPTER 9

KEEPING A KNITTING JOURNAL

Susan S. Jorgensen

Your eyes foresaw my actions;
in your book all are written down . . .

—Psalm 139:16

As far as we know, there is no beatitude that begins with the words, "Blessed are those who journal. . . ." Keeping a journal to record or document when and to whom you give away the shawls that you knit, whether it be as an individual or a community, is not a "requirement" of the shawl-knitting ministry. Nor is everyone interested in maintaining a journal. Those who do are not more blessed or fortunate or holier than those who do not.

That said, keeping a journal could be a grace in the present moment and a treasure for the future. Keeping a journal is one way of slowing down and taking time to reflect, to remember, and to honor the gift that the ministry is to both the knitter and the recipient. Your shawl-knitting journal may contain as little as the name of the shawl recipient and the date on which you gave her or him the shawl. If you want to keep a more detailed journal, you may want to include the date that you started the shawl and the various places you worked on it. Just for fun. Just for you. In this way, it's just like any other journal you keep.

Consider keeping track of how many shawls you give away. I love numbers, so this has a certain appeal for me. Several women I know have knit more than one hundred shawls. If it takes the average knitter twenty hours to knit a shawl, that amounts to two thousand hours of knitting, which is comparable to a forty-hour-a-week job for an entire year! They have earned my admiration.

You may want even more detail in your journal. You could record some of your thoughts and prayers, musings and memories, as you knit your shawls. If you know the person who is receiving the shawl, tell the story of how you were inspired to knit this shawl. Any or all of this could be in the form of a letter in your journal. I am currently knitting shawls for each of my mother's three cousins, who are all in their seventies. The female line in this family is very strong; they did many things together and kept in close contact even as they moved and married, had children, and grew old together. As I knit, I am remembering all the stories my mom shared with me about her cousins when they were younger. I am also recalling the annual summer reunions at the family farm on Lake Ontario when every one of the aunts and uncles, cousins and grandchildren would come together for one magical day. We ate all our favorite foods, went on hayrides through the apple orchard, played croquet on the biggest lawn I had ever seen. The girl cousins of a certain age always sneaked into the rambling old red barn and told secrets for hours. The memories slip from stitch to stitch, as my prayer flows with the rhythm of the needles. The experience has been tender and rich, one that I will record and pass on to my children. How often the giver of a gift is blessed at least as much as its recipient.

If you are artistic or have been thinking about trying your hand at drawing, painting, or collage, you may want to begin a knitting journal that has fewer words and more visuals. The visuals could include one of the wrappers from the yarn that you used, pieces of the yarn, perhaps a photo of the shawl or its recipient, if you know the person and that person is comfortable having his or her picture taken. If you are keeping this type of journal, consider using a spiral-bound notebook that has a heavier weight paper. I use a notebook with 80 lb (36 kg), acid-free, smooth cream drawing paper that measures 7" x 10" (18 cm x 25 cm). The paper supports all sorts of things—watercolor, ink, glue, pastels, charcoal. Local art supply stores will carry these types of journals. A good store will have qualified people who can answer your questions and steer you in the right direction. Whatever you choose, make sure that the paper is acid free (archival quality). You may want to spray each completed sheet with an acrylic coating to preserve your work; if you are gluing bits of yarn on the page, the coating will help keep the yarn from fraying as well.

Another way to collect your memories of the shawls is to use a 60 lb (27 kg) 8½" x 11" (22 cm x 28 cm) card stock that you can slip into a plastic sleeve and store in a loose-leaf binder. Using this paper, you can easily create a sheet for each shawl on a computer, complete with display type and color graphics if you have a color printer.

Any of these methods will serve as a fine alternative if you are interested in creating a journal that contains more than words. Here is one sample:

Community records are also important. Inevitably leadership changes, elders pass on, and stories get lost. A journal can be an invaluable way to preserve the communal history. Our knitting circle keeps a simple list. We have a pre-numbered sheet that we keep in a plastic sleeve that fits into a loose-leaf notebook. We ask each knitter to record the date, the name of the shawl recipient, and a brief blessing for the person. It looks like this:

L et us celebrate the people for whom these shawls have been knit:

Date and Name:

		Blessing/Prayer
1.	10/02 Carolyn and baby son	birth
2.	10/02 Cammie	terminal cancer
3.	10/02 Vi	cancer
4.	10/02 Paul's wife	breast cancer
5.	10/02 Maureen	lupus
6.	11/02 Jean Szinke	good health.
7.	11/02 Elaine	during a time of deep loss
8.	11/02 Jean's mother	loss of child
9.	11/02 Donna	loving daughter
10.	11/02 Patricia	loving daughter
11.	11/02 Jen Jill	Jen Daughter in Law
12.	11/02 Joanna	moving transition.
13.	11/10 Peggy E.	Spiritual
14.	11/10 Peggy S.	STRESS
15.	12/10 Fay	Gratitude
16.	12/10	Young girl whose mother is ill

Whether you are creating a personal journal or a community record, feel free to experiment. Savoring our stories is one way to extend the experience of contemplative presence, to savor each shawl, to remember, to enjoy. May the Spirit fill you with freedom and inspiration.

PART FOUR

BINDING OFF

CHAPTER 10

GIVING AWAY
A SHAWL

Susan S. Jorgensen

O, heart, make your wish—
the gifts are ready, the King is waiting with open arms.[31]

—RUMI

For me, giving away a shawl is the hardest part of this ministry. I have pondered this difficulty since I gave away my first one. The shyness of my childhood overtakes me and I am often tongue-tied and inarticulate as I present these gifts of my hands and heart. Not because I am attached to the shawl. Not because I am afraid the person to whom I am giving it will not like it. Words become empty vessels even as my heart is bursting and full. These shawls are among the most intimate gifts I have ever given to anyone because they are a concrete expression of my prayer, a tangible manifestation of a lasting, intimate encounter with Mystery.

After all the hours of knitting, it seems only reasonable to put some thought into how you want to give away the shawl you have made. You may want to consider the place where you'll give it away, how you present the shawl, what blessing you may want to give the person or what you might want to say, and when it is the "right" time to give the gift. I have a shawl that I finished knitting for a young widow eleven months ago. It sits, waiting, carefully tucked into my yarn basket, for its appointed time. Do not assume that just because you have tied on the last piece of fringe and knotted every one, you must run out and give it to the designated recipient.

All work of our hearts and hands has a gestation period that reveals itself at its chosen time. The key ingredient in knowing when a shawl's time has come is to trust that the true author of this process is active Mystery. Refrain from imposing your will upon it. I trust that you will be both surprised and delighted by the outcome. How many times have you received something—not when you thought it would come or had carefully planned that it would happen—but at a different time, a time that proved to be just the right moment? Susan's way of trusting that the person for whom she is knitting a shawl will be revealed in time (even though she may not know who that is as she begins) is based on the same premise.

When the time has come to give a shawl away, you might find it helpful to do some reflection. If you keep a journal, consider writing down your thoughts, whether this is your first, fiftieth, or hundredth completed shawl. You might also reflect on how you want to be with the shawl recipient—this is about the quality of presence. Presence seems to be something we talk about a lot and one of those qualities of being that we assume we just know how to do. I believe that presence requires practice, and I do not believe we ever arrive at the end of the experience of being present; it seems to have no bottom or any limit. Mindfulness and prayerfulness are two important qualities of presence to practice as you give away the shawls you knit.

Mindfulness

Mindfulness involves being aware of what we are doing in the present moment. Buddhist practice sets forth five basic precepts for living, outlined by Thich Nhat Hanh in his 1993 book, *For a Future to Be Possible: Commentaries on the Five Wonderful Precepts*. He describes these precepts as "mindfulness training." It isn't my intent to repeat or to interpret this master's work here, but simply to say a few things about the quality of being mindful as it relates to the shawl-knitting ministry.

To be mindful is to be attentive to who we are. There is no limit to mindfulness. Mindfulness leads us to self-knowledge. When we discover ourselves as the amazing beings that we truly are, something shifts in us. We become more able to appropriate the truth of who we are at a cellular level. Mindfulness is our "I am" to ourselves, to others, and to God. We find the wisdom to say to the One who is, "You created me in your image. *I am.* You wonderfully made me. *I am.* You have called me by name. *I am.* You hold me in the palm of your hand. *I am.* You provide for me. *I am.* You shelter me from the noonday sun. *I am.* You love me. *I am.*"

This "I am" is not grandiose or pompous. Rather, it is an "I am" that flows quietly from us out of humble awe for God's generous gift of this part of creation—ourselves. It is this "I am" that we knit into our shawls, perhaps without even knowing that it is happening, and it is this "I am" that sits in near-transparent fashion with the recipients of these shawls.

When we are truly alive, everything we do or touch is a miracle. To practice mindfulness is to return to life in the present moment.[32]

THICH NHAT HANH

. . . singing psalms, hymns and spiritual songs with gratitude in your hearts to God.

COLOSSIANS 3:16

Prayerfulness

Do not mistake the saying of prayers with the condition of being prayerful. What is prayerfulness? It is so intimately related to mindfulness that to experience one is to experience the other. Mindfulness is an awareness of ourselves. Prayerfulness is an awareness of God. Prayerfulness is our "you are" to God in the quiet of our hearts and in the busyness of our lives.

As with mindfulness, there is no limit to prayerfulness. This awareness births a gentle passion within us—an ache and a longing of the heart—that is palpable. Through our prayerfulness, we become able to say to the One who is, "You created me in your image. *You are.* You wonderfully made me. *You are.* You have called me by name. *You are.* You hold me in the palm of your hand. *You are.* You provide for me. *You are.* You shelter me from the noonday sun. *You are.* You love me. *You are.*" Through our prayerfulness we discover that there is no place that God is not.

Bringing our mindfulness and our prayerfulness to the moment when we present a shawl to another is one way we can be intentional about inviting Mystery into the experience. Prayer is the language of the relationship between the two. One way of honoring the process of knitting a shawl as we prepare to give it away is through heartfelt expressions of gratitude, through the prayers that we pray in the inner recesses of our hearts and those we pray aloud. Take the time to gaze—to look long and lovingly at the shawl you are giving away; notice how it feels in your hands as you carefully fold and wrap it; experience the anticipation of meeting its recipient. Your prayer of gratitude in this moment for this moment will fill your heart and be as spontaneous as a child at play:

Be grateful for the ones who taught you to knit. *You are loving, O God.*

Be grateful for the yarn with which you knit, for its color, its texture, its feel in your hands, its weight in your lap. *I am blessed, O God.*

Be grateful for the act of knitting as it draws you more deeply into Mystery. *You are generous, O God.*

Be grateful for the person who is receiving this shawl, whether or not you know him or her. Your ministry would be quite empty without the presence of someone who welcomes your gift. *I am blessed, O God.*

Giving Away a Shawl

Giving away a shawl has certain ritual elements to it. Many people develop formal rituals for this; others are more casual. What you choose to do on a given occasion will depend on whether you are giving a shawl to someone you will be meeting face-to-face, mailing it to someone far away, or sending it to a hospital or halfway home or other institution for a person you have never met. Your own sense of what is meaningful and comfortable for you and for the one you are honoring, comforting, and supporting will also play a part in the choices you make. Let's look at some of these elements.

Presentation. Often, shawls are wrapped in tissue paper and tied with a strand of leftover yarn. You might include a simple one-page history of the shawl-knitting ministry (found on page 147) so that the shawl recipient has a sense of the continuity and connection that his or her shawl represents. You might want to include a written blessing or share with the person the page from your knitting journal that tells the story of that particular shawl.

Ritual is one of the oldest ways to mobilize the power of community for healing. It makes the caring of the community visible, tangible, real.[33]

RACHEL NAOMI
REMEN, M.D.

Prayer. If you are part of a knitting circle, chances are that your circle will pray over the shawl you are giving away. If you do not belong to a knitting circle, you might want to consider praying a blessing over the shawl aloud or silently before you give it away. Once you have blessed the shawl, you might also want to pray a prayer of gratitude for having the opportunity to knit this shawl for this person.

Face-to-face. Once the shawl has been unwrapped, you may want to drape it over the recipient's shoulders. This part of giving away a shawl is my favorite. You will need to gauge your comfort level and that of the person receiving the shawl. You may not be comfortable draping the shawl over someone's shoulders; the person to whom you give the shawl may not be comfortable having you do that. Trust your intuition and your knowledge of yourself and the other. If the comfort level is not there for one of you, the moment will be more awkward than moving.

When there is mutual comfort, this act becomes an expression of intimacy that, for me, is always poignant and expresses mindfulness and prayerfulness in a way that words cannot. Making eye contact deepens the experience for me. The act isn't complicated and it doesn't require elaborate preparation. There is something moving about witnessing the way a person's body responds, how it opens itself to receive the shawl, and about watching the shawl settle itself around a person's shoulders in a silent, graceful drape.

Not long ago I was talking with a friend for whom I knit a shawl in the spring of 2001; it was one of my first. When I gave it to her, I carefully draped it over her shoulders, letting it fall to her sides. During a recent conversation I was telling her that I had finished a shawl for a mutual friend whose brother had died and that I was going to be putting it in the mail soon. My friend said,

"Please don't do that. Please find a way to give it to her in person. The one thing that I remember the most when you gave me the shawl was how it felt when you put it on me. Now, I can't put it on without thinking about you. Whenever I wrap it around myself, you are there with me in memory and in spirit." God's presence reveals itself in the simplest of gestures. Smoke and bells and chanting have invoked God's name through the ages for nearly every major religion, but a simple shawl wrapped tenderly around another in a gesture of love and gratitude has the same effect.

Another option you might choose is to read a prepared blessing, such as the ones found in this book on pages 115–134. You could also pray a blessing extemporaneously, trusting the Spirit to fill you with the right words. You might even give the person a written blessing. If these sorts of things don't work for you, don't use them. The key here is to honor and respect your own way of doing things.

Communal rituals. Sometimes a person receives a shawl in gratitude for service to a community. We recently presented a shawl to the president of a board on which I serve, to acknowledge her years of leadership. The members of the board gathered around her as she stood in the center of the circle, presented the shawl to her, and one member draped it around her. We placed our hands upon her as we each offered individual blessing prayers.

Some groups create healing rituals whereby the person who is suffering first prays, either aloud or silently, about hopes for healing. The group then blesses the shawl in unison. One member places the shawl on the recipient's shoulders and then each person lays hands on the recipient, invoking, either aloud or silently, God's healing presence upon the person. Similar rituals work for birthdays, weddings, anniversaries, and rites of passage. In those cases, the

I will bless you as long as I live; I will lift up my hands, calling on your name.

PSALM 63:4

recipient prays aloud his or her hopes and dreams for the coming year, event, or experience, and the group prays their support as they invite God to be with that person.

Use your own intuition and develop a style for giving away shawls that suits you. Whether or not you know the person who is to receive the shawl, whether it is sent or delivered in person, whether it is two people who gather or a group, I believe the key ingredients to any occasion of presenting a shawl are:

1. Mindfulness.

2. Prayerfulness.

3. Respect and consideration for the person or community giving away the shawl and for the person receiving it. An imposed prayer or ritual, no matter how beautiful or carefully prepared and executed, will fall flat if it offends or creates discomfort.

CHAPTER 11

RECEIVING AND WEARING A SHAWL

Susan S. Jorgensen

No ear has ever heard, no eye ever seen, any God
but you doing such deeds for those who wait for him.

—Isaiah 64:3

The gift of a shawl is not usually something for which you can prepare yourself. Often a shawl comes when you least expect it and when you most need it. Isn't this often how the Spirit works? I regularly counsel my directees to be open to God's endless, creative surprise. Receiving a shawl is an experience that cannot be absorbed completely in one moment; it draws us into a silent, deep place that cannot be adequately expressed by any combination of words. Wearing a shawl is an experience that satisfies what seems to be a basic need to feel loved and cared for, surrounded and safe. Both occasions lead us into the heart of inexpressible Mystery; it may be helpful to look briefly at each.

Receiving a Shawl

What is it that you receive when you receive a shawl? What—or who—is it that you welcome? I am reminded of the passages in Christian scripture in which Jesus says, "The one who welcomes/receives me welcomes/receives the one who sent me" (Matthew 10:40 and John 13:20). When you receive a shawl, you welcome the one(s) who knit it for you, whether you know them or not. Their presence, their prayer, their intention is woven through the fibers of the yarn. And by welcoming the one or ones who knit your shawl, you also welcome Mystery. Real. Tangible. Visible. In thousands of knit and purl stitches that weave themselves into a beautiful whole.

What is it that you receive when you receive a shawl? You receive a garment that proclaims peace—peace over you, peace under you, peace within you, peace around you. We cannot knit and hold a gun. We cannot knit and strike another. You receive a shawl that has been knit in love—love that is freely given for its own sake. I don't know of a soul who knits shawls for material gain or recognition. The people I know who knit are passionate about loving and seek only to express that love through their craft. You receive a garment that has been filled with healing intentions and comfort, a garment that seeks to console and give solace, a garment that celebrates and affirms, a garment that showers abundant blessings upon its wearer from the compassionate heart of its knitter.

What is it that you receive when you receive a shawl? You receive membership into a circle that has no boundaries, a circle with a momentum that continues to ripple out into the global community. The sum of it has become far greater than any of the people and parts that have played its midwives. The shawl-knitting ministry has a life of its own. Wear a shawl in a public place, and you will be noticed. You will be asked, "Isn't that one of those shawls?" "Who knit it for you?" "How can I get one?"

In a time when war is destroying what we hold dear and the world is in chaos, you receive peace that you may be peace. You receive love that you may be love. You receive healing that you may heal. You receive affirmation that you may affirm. Be mindful. Be prayerful. Welcome the Mystery.

Wearing a Shawl

Human beings love being wrapped. The activity touches a deep chord within. I sit at my computer composing this chapter, wrapped in a luxurious, deep purple shawl that is a combination of sheep and llama wool. Small glass seed beads are scattered randomly, snugly sewn into the tiny waves of the K3, P3 pattern; they catch the light as I move and stretch. This shawl is incredibly soft; it clings to all the curves of my body. As I pull it around me tight, I am continually amazed by the ability of this garment to yield to the shape of my body. I feel safe; I feel held; I feel loved. I believe two things are happening here: a very primitive and early need is being touched and satisfied, and the prayer of another is seeping into the fiber of my being.

Among the first experiences a baby has after emerging from the womb is being wrapped in "swaddling clothes." "Swaddling" is one of those words that we rarely hear or speak, unless you happen to be at Christmas services when the Gospel of St. Luke is proclaimed. The word comes from an Anglo-Saxon word, *swæthel*, and it is narrowly defined as those clothes that are wrapped around a newborn.

I suspect that this experience stays with us at the cellular level for our entire lives. One of my favorite mothering experiences was of tucking in my children. We never skipped that part of our bedtime ritual. I don't know if they ever

In a society . . . where relationships and the sense of community are fragmented, it may be time to place some emphasis on the blessings of receiving.[34]

PATRICIA LORING

*Behind and before
you encircle me
and rest your hand
upon me.*

PSALM 139:5

knew that I also sneaked quietly into their rooms in the last hours of the evening when the night had grown cold to tuck them in again—to straighten the covers, to smooth the locks of sleep-damp hair across their foreheads, to feel their baby breath across my hand. I have not lost the love of being tucked in myself when I am sick or sleeping on the couch; my children often do for me as I have done for them. The care and tenderness with which they wrap the blanket around me soothes and quiets me. In my drowsy state, I can only smile deeply as their love washes through me.

When you wrap yourself in your shawl, you wrap the prayer of another around your shoulders and across your chest. Do not doubt that prayer has gone into every stitch of every row of your shawl, no matter who has knit it for you. Tuck it around you tenderly and with awe. Not long ago, several of us were in a small group talking, of course, about one of our favorite topics—knitting shawls. One of the women had developed her own intricate, beautiful pattern for shawls. I was ready to abandon the K3, P3 pattern—hers is that gorgeous—until she told me that each one takes her forty hours to complete. While I would not say she considers herself a spiritual neophyte, neither would I say she puts herself in a class with spiritual masters. She is down-to-earth, very funny, real.

She was offhanded and chuckling when she exclaimed, "Whoever gets one of the shawls I make is going to have to have someone else pray over it. I just watch TV when I knit." I smiled. Perhaps it is because I know and admire her, perhaps it was something I picked up in her voice, I'm not really sure. Whatever it was, I could sense the fullness of the prayer that went into her shawls. Prayer just can't help itself to be anything but present in this activity.

Maybe it isn't always prayer of a conventional sort, but I believe prayer seeps through our fingers, into the yarn, and around our needles each time we pick up a shawl to knit on it.

Do not doubt the power of the prayer that is present in your shawl. After returning home one September afternoon to recover from a particularly grueling medical procedure, I curled up in a lounge chair on my deck in a patch of sun, a shawl wrapped around me. A friend had knit this one for me to celebrate a healing in our relationship. The prayer flowed—no, burst forth and spilled out—cascading over my tired and aching body. I felt a warmth that was more than the warmth from just a garment; it was a pulsating energy that spoke to me of God's presence supporting me, of angel wings around me, of healing energy flowing through me.

So much has been written about the power of prayer to heal and transform, but there is so much we don't yet understand. Studies continue to tell us that groups of patients for whom people pray recover faster and with fewer complications than the control groups for whom no one is praying. Scientists say that the data is both compelling and inexplicable. I pray that you are able to fall into trust, to open yourself to the power of the prayer with which you are enfolded each time you reach for your shawl. Be mindful. Be prayerful. Experience the Mystery.

Many traditions provide prayers for the occasion of putting on a sacred garment. Below you will find several prayers that are appropriate for the times when you wrap yourself in your shawl.

For she said, "If I touch even his garments, I shall be made well."

MARK 5:28 RSV

Intention for the Wearing of a Shawl

WAYNE TEASDALE

O Blessed One, transform us (all sentient beings) into that infinite Love you are, and let us always radiate that Love to you, to one another, and all those we meet unto eternal life.

A Blessing for the Wearer of a Shawl

ADAPTED FROM A CELTIC PRAYER BY ROBERT JONAS

May the blessing of light be on you,
    light without and light within
        and light inside the darkness within.
    May the blessed sunlight shine upon you
    and warm your heart till it glows,
        like a great peat fire, so that strangers may come
        and warm themselves; and that friends may come.
    And may the light shine out of the eyes of you,
    like a candle set in the windows of a house,
        bidding the wanderer to come in out of the storm.
    And may the blessing of the rain be on you—
        the soft, sweet rain.
    May it fall upon your spirit so that the seedlings of light
    in your shadow may spring up,

and shed their sweetness on the air.
And may the blessing of the great rains be on you,
that they beat upon your spirit and wash it fair and clean,
and leave there many a shining pool,
and sometimes a star.
And may the blessing for the earth be on you—
the great round earth
who carries all; the great round earth
whose suffering has already become radiant.
May you ever have a kindly greeting for people
you pass as you are going along the roads.
And now may the Lord bless you, and bless you kindly,
your kin and all creatures.

A Hindu Prayer

TAKEN FROM THE BRHADAARANYAKA UPANISHAD
CONTRIBUTED BY DR. A. V. SRINIVASAN

असतोमा सत्गमया तमसोमा ज्योतिर्गमया
म्रुत्योर्मा अम्रुतं गमया ॐ शानति: शानति: शानति:

Asathomaa sathgamayaa thamasomaa jyothirgamayaa
Mrthyormaa amrutham gamayaa Om shanthih shanthih shanthihi

Lead me from the unreal to the real, lead me from darkness to light
Lead me from death to eternal life, Om peace, peace, peace

Jewish Shawl Blessing

PSALM 104: 1–2
TAKEN FROM SHABBAT MORNING SERVICE
CONTRIBUTED BY ANNA ROSE AND MONTE SUGARMAN

בָּרְכִי נַפְשִׁי אֶת־יהוה! יהוה אֱלֹהַי, גָּדַלְתָּ מְּאֹד!
הוֹד וְהָדָר לָבָשְׁתָּ, עֹטֶה־אוֹר כַּשַּׂלְמָה, נוֹטֶה שָׁמַיִם כַּיְרִיעָה.

Bar-chi naf-shi et A-do-nai.
Praise the Eternal One, O my soul!
O God, You are very great!

Arrayed in glory and majesty, You wrap Yourself in light as with a garment, and stretch out the heavens like a curtain.[35]

—from *Gates of Prayer for Shabbat and Weekdays*

The commentary in the *Kol Haneshamab–Shabbat Vehagim* states that "God's wrapping in light becomes Israel's enlightened wrapping at the outset of a new day."[36] May it be so for each of us.

PART FIVE

STORIES AND
PRAYERS

CHAPTER 12
STORIES OF WITNESS

Susan S. Izard

God made man because he loves stories.[37]
—ELIE WEISEL

$\mathscr{E}$ver since the beginning of humankind, stories have been powerful tools for passing on information and wisdom. Children adore stories and ask us to tell them over and over again. Hebrew and Christian scriptures use stories as a way to enlighten, delight, and surprise. The stories of the shawl-knitting ministry are no less powerful. They touch our hearts, and speak to us of the transformative nature of this kind of ministry.

The majority of the stories about the shawl-knitting ministry that I have heard over the years have been personal. People who have received shawls from my church have sent notes or letters of thanks to our circle. It is remarkable to know something as simple as knitting a shawl can be such a comfort. One woman wrote: "Although I have heard of ministries like yours, I was unprepared for the depth of my reaction to being a recipient—I was overwhelmed by the feelings of love and comfort I felt as I wrapped the shawl around my shoulders. I cherish it. Everything about it is comforting—the muted colors, the softness of the yarn, the ample size that engulfs me, the calmness I feel when I begin to pray with it on. But most of all I cherish it because it was given to me by others of faith—your ministry has truly been a blessing for me." Cards like this have been a blessing for us. They have given words to the purpose of our knitting. They have reinforced our sense of God's presence and love conveyed through the ministry, and remind us how important it is to care for others.

Oral stories have been equally powerful. In the fall of 2001, Janet Bristow and I met each other and decided to host a gathering for shawl-knitting ministries from around the state of Connecticut. We gathered to knit together, pray together, eat together, and share the story of the ministry. Toward the end of the day, an elderly woman stood up to share her story. Several years ago, she told us, her husband had been killed in an accident. They had been married for over fifty years, and his death had devastated her. She was overcome by grief. Her anguish was so intense that members of her church became concerned about her. They wanted to let her know how much they cared about her, and so a few women went to her home and presented her with a shawl.

The shawl was an enormous comfort to this woman. She never went anywhere without it. She even slept with it wrapped around her shoulders. Friends began to wonder if she would ever wear anything else. The shawl became a significant part of her healing process. One day, she was finally ready to clean out her husband's closet. All went well until she came across the sweater she had knit for him when they were in college. Sobbing and hugging the sweater to her

---

When we tell our stories to one another we discover that we share the same joys and tragedies, the same ambiguities and struggles.[38]

SUE MONK KIDD

chest, she wrapped her shawl tightly around herself. The comfort of the shawl was the only thing that kept her from completely falling apart. "The shawl was my salvation," she told us.

Over the years, it has become clear that the creative spirit that gave birth to the shawl-knitting ministry continues to flourish. One of the greatest delights of the ministry has been hearing from people who have adapted the original idea to fit their needs. One friend, who is a spiritual director, told me how she knit herself a prayer shawl from the Sufi tradition. During a long discernment process, she came up with the specifications for her shawl. She wrote, "I chose white because that color is commonly worn for prayer within the Sufi Order. The Mevlevi Dervishes wear white for their turning, or 'whirling.' American Sufis often have white shawls made of wool or cashmere. There is some debate about what 'Sufi' means, whether coming from an Arabic word for wool, or from the Greek *Sophia,* wisdom. . . . The shawl has come to have rich meaning for me as I learn more about the Sufi path; as I think about my own role as spiritual director, liturgical healer, and pastoral visitor; and as I become more at ease with appropriating authority toward my upcoming ordination as an Interfaith Minister. The shawl symbolizes my comfort, my personal vestment, my wedding dress. It is God's gift to me that incidentally was made by my own hands." This story of prayer and discernment around a shawl attests to the power shawls offer us when we are enveloped in them. Through these shawls, God touches us and invites us to become a part of God's great sacred story of life.

Shawls have also inspired liturgical practices, particularly prayers that people have written to use when knitting and giving away the shawls. Others have integrated shawls in worship services. A few days after September 11, 2001, Cathy Murtha, DW, told me that her nephew had been killed when the World Trade Center collapsed. He left behind a wife and four young children.

. . . we speak God's wisdom, mysterious, hidden, which God predetermined before the ages for our glory.

1 CORINTHIANS 2:7

The wind blows
where it wills,
and you hear
the sound of it,
but you do not
know whence it
comes from or
whither it goes.

JOHN 3:8 RSV

She wanted to give shawls to both her sister (who was the young man's mother) and her nephew's widow, but did not have any that were finished and wondered if the shawl-knitting ministry at my church had any extra shawls. Before sending the shawls that we picked for the women, Cathy wrote the "Prayer for Comfort" (page 122). She shared it with me in thanks for giving her the shawls. I was struck by the power of her prayer and started to include it with almost all the shawls that we gave away. It soon became clear that the prayer was touching people as much as the shawls were. Cathy's prayer has become an integral part of the ministry. I even used it for the benediction for a prayer service we held after my father died. Very spontaneously, the senior pastor and I wrapped ourselves in our prayer shawls and read the "Prayer for Comfort" at the end of the service. It was a moment of grace for all who attended and a true witness to God's encompassing love and embracing heart in times of mourning and overwhelming grief.

Many groups have embraced the creative spirit of the ministry and personalized it to meet their own needs. One spiritual director and Episcopal priest sent me the announcement that she put in her church newsletter as she was beginning the shawl-knitting ministry in her church in Texas. The announcement read:

"YarnWorks: Ministry of the Fibers will hold its first meeting on Saturday, January 27, from 2:00 to 4:00 P.M. in Room 200, Saint Mark's Episcopal Church. The purpose of the ministry is to create prayer shawls, blankets, caps or other garments as an outward and visible sign of the mystical reality of prayer that knits our souls together in God and Christ. These garments are given to the nursing mothers, the sick, homebound, poor and elderly in our midst to comfortably remind them that they are present to us and bound to us in community even in their loneliness, illness, pain or exhaustion. Its secondary purpose is to ensure that fiber arts are taught to younger generations so they are not lost. Any person (male, female, old or young) who knits, crochets or spins (or wants to learn how) is invited to participate. In addition to fiber artists, YarnWorks is soliciting musicians, poets, readers or storytellers who would like to share their talents to come and serenade those who are working with their hands."

Another spiritual director who works with inmates as well as in a local parish sent this note: "Our parish knitting ministry continues to thrive. We're making baby blankets for children born to prisoners as well as prayer shawls. Next weekend we will have anointing of the sick during the masses and will offer prayer shawls to those anointed, adding our own personal touch to the sacrament." In the same spirit, another church has a knitting group for ages nine and up. The children knit small white baptismal shawls for the infants who are baptized. The pastor wraps each infant in his or her baptismal shawl after the baptism.

Stories from countries around the world have been particularly exciting to receive. The knitting circle at my church was delighted to hear from a women's organization from the Church of England that had begun knitting shawls. Their first shawl went to a vicar who had been sick for many months. She loved the shawl and felt encompassed in God's embracing arms while wrapped in the shawl. It is amazing to us that the shawl-knitting ministry has spread to so many places and been adapted to meet the needs of so many groups.

Church groups are not the only ones who have adopted the ministry and infused it with their own creative ideas. Soon after the ministry began, a minister who is a breast cancer survivor saw the shawls and learned that they were being given to women with breast cancer. She took the idea of the shawls to her local breast cancer support group. They decided to knit a shawl for every woman who entered the group as a way of nurturing and supporting her. The

If I speed away on the wings of the dawn, if I dwell beyond the ocean, even there your hand will be guiding me, your right hand holding me fast.

PSALMS 139:9–10 NJB

knitting spread to other breast cancer support groups in the region, and the women began to give shawls to doctors working on the oncology floors of local hospitals. These doctors give away the shawls to their patients. The word continued to spread to the national level of this breast cancer support group, and now breast cancer patients are knitting for other patients all over the country.

Another organization that works to abolish domestic violence is knitting 1,200 shawls for the mothers and sisters of women who have been murdered because of domestic violence. The shawls, named for the founder of the organization, are a way of honoring her as well as offering compassion for victims of domestic violence.

These are just a few of the stories of witness that we have heard about over the past few years. As the shawl-knitting ministry continues to widen its circle, many more stories will touch our hearts and amaze us. As you become a part of this ministry and its story, it is our hope that your heart will be open to the creative spirit of Wisdom as she invites you to knit and care for others. It is our hope that you will be open to the transforming power of God's love through the witness of the shawls and stories, and that you will spread the word by telling others about the ministry and teaching others to knit. In that way, more of God's children will know God's love through the warmth of a shawl. This common experience of God's presence will become an avenue to peace and respect for one another regardless of our race or religion. May your knitting be blessed.

Beloved, we are God's children now; what we shall be has not yet been revealed.

1 JOHN 3:2

Within a year of that knitting class, my priorities changed when my first child, Jonathan, was born. Two years later I was three months pregnant when I went on a family vacation to St. Martin with my son, parents, and grand-mother. While sitting on the beach with my mother, I noticed that I was spotting. I panicked and went quickly to the hospital. The doctors warned us, "It doesn't look good; you'll miscarry sometime during the night." Shaken by the prognosis, we decided that we would all be more comfortable if we spent the night back at our hotel. Settling in for the long vigil, my mother gave me her shawl, which my husband's aunt had made for her. I placed it upon my womb and began praying to the Blessed Mother with my mother and grandmother. I did not miscarry during the night! The following day, I went into town for an ultrasound and there was my child! Wiggling and thriving! He miraculously swept his hand across his face as if to say, "Hi!" From that moment, the doctors advised me to rest to protect my unborn son, whom we named Nicholas.

In late 1997, after graduating from the Women's Leadership Institute (WLI), I went back to the task of completing the unfinished sweater. My efforts were to no avail and I became frustrated. I switched to knitting what I called small dish towels. I made dozens, giving them to friends and relatives. One day as I was watching a television talk show, I was moved by a woman who took her love of cooking chicken soup and turned it into a business of making and delivering it to those who were ill. Taking what I had learned and experienced from the WLI and the television program, I felt challenged and called upon to look into myself and see what talents I could share with others.

I was inspired to knit a shawl, but not just any shawl. I wanted to create something that was a gift of myself to others. The pattern of knitting in threes, tying on the tassels in significant numbers, and paying attention to the symbolism attached to the various colors came to me in prayer.

Through WLI, I met Janet Bristow. We both belong to a close circle of "sisters" that meets on a monthly basis. I brought my prototype shawl with me and used it as part of a guided meditation at our January 1998 meeting that Janet hosted in her home. When she looked at the shawl, she suggested adding beads, charms, and trinkets to make it more meaningful, and offering prayers and blessings into each stitch and over every shawl. The first shawl that I created was for one of our "sisters" who was going through a divorce. Each woman in our circle wrapped the shawl around herself and offered silent prayers and blessings into it for our hurting "sister."

When I gave my "sister" her shawl, I was astonished by the impact it had on her. She was deeply touched by the thought that each stitch had been prayed over as it was created and that each of her "sisters" had poured their blessings into the shawl. She immediately felt the power and energy of the shawl.

The synchronicity of the shawl-knitting ministry continues to amaze me. I experience Mother God speaking through this ministry and comforting her children. The ministry supports the growing presence of the Divine Feminine energy and influence throughout our world, balances the masculine, and counteracts the destructive power of all energy that is out of control. I feel blessed to be a vehicle chosen for this ministry.

To my story, Janet adds, "This ministry has evolved in ways that we could never have predicted. As soon as we started knitting these mantles of love and giving them away, it was as if God's Wisdom had swept over us, breathing into us her life-giving, unconditional love. I feel that this energy was waiting for us, urging us on, calling us to be her hands, to reach out to her children in the difficult as well as joyful times so that they could become consciously aware of her presence in their lives. People need to know this more than ever because this world has become such a difficult, scary place."

CHAPTER 14

PRAYERS FOR
THE SEASONS OF LIFE:
A COLLECTION

$\mathcal{S}$t. Paul counsels Christians to "pray without ceasing" (1 Thessalonians 5:17). One day in the early spring of 2002, a colleague asked me to write a prayer that she could share with her eleven-year-old great-niece, Jordan, who was blind. My colleague had knit her a shawl, attaching stars and assorted shapes to the fringe to give her something to touch. I was deeply moved by Ann's invitation, and the Spirit stirred strongly—it was one of those moments when my soul could feel a seed being planted deep within. If my colleague needed a prayer for a particular occasion, I felt certain that others had that need, too.

Thus, I trace the origin of this book back to a child who lived passionately and bravely fought many physical difficulties, and to her aunt who asked for a child's prayer that would accompany the shawl she had knit for her. I am humbled by the winding, ingenious threads that the Spirit knits to connect us all. Jordan died unexpectedly not long after her great-aunt wrapped her in a beautiful shawl of love and healing, and prayed with her. Her life continues to touch others in many different ways; in my own, as the inspiration for this book.

Throughout history, prayer has had the power to unite as well as separate. It has been misused countless times by the world's religions to sustain war and sanctify bloodshed. At this time in our human story perhaps as never before because of the proliferation of so many weapons of mass destruction, we need to lean into the unifying power of prayer. The prayers we offer here are a modest beginning. They come from many traditions. Please feel free to use them as they apply to your own situations. Give credit to the individual authors and pause to offer a word of thanksgiving for the Spirit who has moved in them through word.

Knitting Life

Kent Ira Groff

gather this garment
of silence about me,
stillness that used to be
threatening,
its needles
of fear lurking,
probing wounds of my past,
scars to my psyche.

Now in the hands of Love
these needles have knitted
a silence so beautiful
that nothing
can hurt. I draw skeins
of silence with this healing
garment about me,
as its stitches permeate
the crevices of my soul
whispering, Peace.
Be still—and know:
Now all that would harm you
is knitted to warm you.

Prayer for Healing

CATHLEEN O'MEARA MURTHA, DW

In the beginning, creating God, you formed my being.
You knit me together in my mother's womb.
To my flesh and blood you gave the breath of life.

O Loving One, renew me this day in your love
Grant me life as gift of your faithfulness;
Grant me light to journey by;
Grant me hope to sustain me.

May this mantle be for me a sign of your healing presence.
May it warm me when I am weary;
May it surround me with ease of my suffering;
May it encircle me with caring when I am in pain.

O Christ who healed the broken in body and spirit,
Be with me and all who suffer this day.
Be with the doctors, nurses, technicians, chaplains and all who
Care for the sick.
Be with families and friends of those abiding with and comforting the sick.
May your gentle, yet strong touch reach out to heal all the broken and hurting
People and places in our world.

Healing for Broken Bones and Other Things

RACHEL HARRIS

In my hand
The knitting needles
Called the energy
Down from the heavens
Wound it 'round the yarn
In intricate pattern
Lacing it through the weave
Turning it into healing.
Straw into gold
Wool into light
Emanating
From every loop
Filled with my prayers
Whispered from my heart.

Please receive this shawl.
Curl it around you
Close it over you
Like child's play
And enter into
The warm, dark, quiet
Stillness.

There you can rest
Wait for healing
Make friends with time.

Let your body
Breathe in
The secrets of the shawl.
Feel the light
Reach into your bones
Mending, knitting,
Weaving them together
In a new way.
Birthing a new body
Creating a new future.

For Jordan
1991–2002

SUSAN S. JORGENSEN

When you wrap yourself in this shawl, bless
yourself in the name of the Father who loves you,
and of the Son who is your brother and your friend,
and of the Holy Spirit who guides your every step.

When I knit this shawl, I prayed many prayers into every stitch:
that this shawl would keep you warm,
make you feel strong,
help you feel better.

May this shawl calm you when you are upset,
remind you that I love you even when I'm not here, and
help you remember that your guardian angel
is always watching over you.

When you wear this shawl, believe with all your heart that:
God is with you every minute of every hour of every day,
Jesus loves you no matter what, and
the Holy Spirit rests upon your shoulder
especially when you are sad or lonely.
May this shawl bring you sweet dreams when you are sleeping.

Amen.

A Prayer for a Parent with Alzheimer's

KATHLEEN O'CONNELL CHESTO

Woven deeply in the stitches
Knitted gently through the strands,
Are the memories—
The funny memories,
The joyful memories,
The painful memories—
The memories of all the love
We have shared.
May you feel the warmth of that love,
Even as the memories escape you.
May you be blessed with the comfort
Of those who hold the memories for you,
Even as you lose their faces and their names.
May this shawl offer security in the confusion,
Courage in the darkness,
Enabling you to walk gently
Into that long night,
Even as I struggle to let you go.

Ariadne's Blessing

JANET BRISTOW

Holy One, whose womb is threaded and waiting,
Guide us to pick up the thread and
Walk the spiral through the dark and difficult passages.

Life Cord, who sustains us as we move to our center,
Give us courage to meet our souls.
Comfort us through our dismantling,
  wrapped in your loving embrace.

Mantle of Love,
Rebirth us with Wisdom
Knit us once again into wholeness.

Prayer for Comfort

CATHLEEN O'MEARA MURTHA, DW

*s you wrap yourself* in this shawl of comfort . . .
May the Mother of Mercy
the Father of Faithfulness and
the Spirit of Compassion
wrap you in their all-encompassing love this day.

May you find comfort
from all that appears too much to bear at this moment
from all that feels as if it might be the breaking point
from all that seems to threaten your peace of heart.

May this shawl be
a shelter for time of overwhelming grief
a shade in times of sorrow too deep for words
a shield from times of unimaginable loss.

May you be comforted
by the presence of those who love and support you
by faith in the eternal Loving One
by the memories of what you hold most dear.

May you be strengthened
    in your daily comings and goings
    in your tentative new beginnings
    in your unfolding new memories.

Blessings of the Angel of Comfort be with you
    and all you love now and forevermore.

A Prayer for One Who Grieves

Susan S. Jorgensen

The ragged edge of grief is one of love's unwelcome partners,
its bent and silent witness carves deep grooves upon the heart . . .

As you move through these long days,
    may you be blessed through
    the wearing of your shawl,
    and carried by your God
    who loves you so.

May those around you comfort you—
may their love soothe your broken heart,
may their care ease your pain,
may their steadfast presence remind you that,
in your grief and in your loss,
you do not mourn alone.

May your tears be gathered by angels,
may your aching heart be eased
by the solace of your God,
may your nagging pain be stilled
by the prayers of those who love you.

May you gently wrap this shawl around you,
may you be surrounded by its love,
enfolded by its prayer,
embraced by its warmth,
and cradled in its womb of softness.

Amen.

For my Daughter to pray, who sits,
Lavender Blue-Shawled,
cradling her newborn daughter . . .

FELICIA B. MCKNIGHT

My whole shawled body
holds the baby
    and the years before
    and the years to come
years and tears
    laughter and coming here and passing through
    the veil between
    then and now, and there and here. . . .
All that is many and every
    becomes one
as my whole shawled body holds the baby
    who is me and she and Thee.

So it is.

Shawl Blessing for a GrandMother

KAY LINDAHL

You are a grandmother now. A GrandMother.
What a beautiful word!

Another thread has been woven into the tapestry of your life.
This shawl is given to you as a blessing for your new role.

As you wrap it around your shoulders,
feel its warmth and sensual touch,
reflect on the awesome gift of new life.

As you wrap it around yourself and the new baby,
feel the love knit into each stitch, enfolding both of you,
enjoy the special bonding of grandmother and grandchild.

Someday this shawl may become a Batman cape, a ball gown,
wings of an airplane or wings of an angel, a fort or a clubhouse,
or who knows what the two of you will imagine.

This shawl is a prayer of love and joy for both of you
as you explore the wonder of your new relationship.

May you always feel blessed by it.
You are a grandmother now. A GrandMother.

A Birthday Blessing

Susan Rakoczy, IHM

A birthday is a day
in which past and future
come together in a moment:
today
to recall the beginning
(maybe even before the beginning)
of life—
the moment when
"beyond nothing"
became
"I am"
in the security of your mother's womb.

Blessed are you
to leap with joy
as gratitude spills from your
heart that you
are
and always will be!

Blessed are you
as your days, weeks, years
(just like the intricate stitches of this shawl)
weave themselves into a pattern
of colors, tints, hues
never known before:
the brightness and light of love
shadows and darkness of sadness and failure
knots of disappointment
loops of friendship and care.

Blessed are you
to know today
as in all days
(but today is special)
that God's sheltering, protecting love
enfolds you
as does this shawl:
wider than your hopes
stronger than your desires
more faithful than your dreams.

Blessed are you always!
Happy Birthday!

Native American Wedding Blessing

ADAPTED FROM THE PAIUTE INDIAN
CONTRIBUTED BY LORETTA WATTS

Now you will feel no rain, for each of you
will be shelter to the other—

Now you will feel no cold, for each of you
will be warmth to the other—

Now there is no more loneliness—

Now you are two persons, but there is only
one life before you.

Go now to your dwelling place, to enter into
the days of your life together—

And may your days be good, and long upon
the earth.

Marriage Blessing

PHILIP GOLDBERG, PH.D.

May the marriage you knit from the loose yarn of your separate lives form a strong, enduring fabric of beauty, warmth, and dignity.

May you give thanks each day that divine love has found its way to you and through you, for each other.

May you rejoice in the privilege of giving love as much as you cherish the feeling of being loved.

May you both wake up each morning with the thought, "What can I give to my beloved today?"

May you two pieces of God walk together to the peace of God.

A Blessing for Your Journey

SUSAN S. JORGENSEN

As you undertake your journey,
may you be blessed through the wearing of your shawl,
and deeply blessed by your God
who loves you so.

May you be blessed with tender savoring—
for the friends and loved ones you leave behind
for the memories that bring a smile
for the stories that bring tears
for all that has been woven into the fabric of your life here.

May you be blessed with steadfast courage—
for the travel you are about to undertake
for the adventure that lies ahead
for the hardships that are part of every journey
and the unexpected twists and turns
that are the spine of life.

May you be blessed with all good things—
with new friends along the way
with safe passage from here to there
with unexpected smiles from strangers and
with offers for help when you need it most.

May you be blessed by Sophia wisdom—
to see God's face in an unfamiliar one
to hear God's voice in birdsong and wind
to recognize God's love in struggle and travail
to embrace God's presence in all that awaits you.

Blessing for a Time of Transition

LORETTA WATTS

All winter long I have had the threads of this tissue in my hands,
and have searched for the ultimate pattern, and though it has become
a tissue of rough, coarse aspect, nevertheless, the threads have been
chosen carefully and according to certain rules.

—VINCENT VAN GOGH, LETTERS

Before squeezing tubes of pigment onto canvas,
Vincent braided yarns to see the effects of complimentary colors
laid side by side. He kept his wools in a box stored beneath
his bed, pulled it out and opened it nights before his small fire,
yellow-gold kindling the blue midnight.

During this time of transition, of darkness, of change,
may your eyes glory in the shades of this shawl.
May your shoulders be warmed by it.
May you be encouraged to pull out the box you have laid away,
open it and choose the colors of your dreams.

May you envision new patterns, as you finger the threads
of your life, their stubble and their sheen.
May you rest, settled into the Master Artist's weave,
for underneath are the Everlasting arms.

Blessings Are Thrown across Our Lives

MARYE GAIL HARRISON

Blessings are thrown across our lives
by the Great Creative Spirit
unfolding the universe,
knitting us together
in community.
Blessings are thrown
across your shoulders
over and over
as you wear this shawl,
blessings woven in
as yarn was thrown over needles
over and over as it was knitted.
May you rest enfolded
in the soft grace
of this continuous thread,
interlocking you with all goodness.

Amen.

Ancient Gaelic Blessing

CONTRIBUTED BY VICTORIA A. COLE-GALO
(WRITTEN ON THE CARDS ATTACHED TO HER SHAWLS)

Deep peace of the quiet earth to you
  Deep peace of the shining stars to you
  Deep peace of the gentle night to you
  Moon and stars pour their healing light to you
  Deep peace to you, deep peace to you.

Our Prayer for You

SUSAN S. JORGENSEN AND SUSAN S. IZARD

May your knitting be blessed.

  May God touch your hands with love
  May God guide your needles with compassion
  May God fill your yarn with Spirit.

  May God touch your heart with peace
  May God guide your soul to freedom
  May God fill your mind with silence.

  May God touch your shawls with warmth
  May God guide your community with joy
  May God fill our world with hope.

  May your knitting be blessed.

NOTES

CELEBRATIONS

1. Patricia Loring, *Listening Spirituality: Volume I, Personal Spiritual Practices Among Friends* (Washington, D. C.: Openings Press, 1997), xiii.

CHAPTER 1

2. Elliott Kronenfeld in Linda Roghaar, and Molly Wolf, eds., *KnitLit: Sweaters and Their Stories . . . and Other Writings About Knitting* (New York: Three Rivers Press, 2002), 126.

3. Susan Gordon Lydon, *The Knitting Sutra: Craft as a Spiritual Practice* (San Francisco: HarperSanFrancisco, 1997), 137.

4. Lewis Newman, ed., *Hasidic Anthology* (New York: Schocken Books, 1963).

CHAPTER 2

5. Lydon, *The Knitting Sutra*, 137.

6. John Main, *Moment of Christ: The Path of Meditation* (New York: Continuum Publishing Company, 1999), 109.

CHAPTER 3

7. Walter Burghardt, "Contemplation: A Long, Loving Look at the Real." *Church*, Winter 1989, 14–18.

8. Lisa R. Myers, *The Joy of Knitting* (Philadelphia: Running Press, 2001), 101.

9. Burghardt, 17.

10. Ibid., 17.

11. Ibid., 17.

12. Ibid., 17.

13. *Meister Eckhart: A Modern Translation.* Trans. Raymond Blakney (New York: Harper Torchbooks, 1961), 206.

14. Burghardt, "Contemplation," 17.

15. Loring, *Listening Spirituality*, 161.

CHAPTER 4

16. Rachel Naomi Remen, M.D., *Kitchen Table Wisdom* (New York: Riverhead Books, 1996), 246.

17. Jane Goodall, *Reason for Hope: A Spiritual Journey* (New York: Warner Books, 2000).

CHAPTER 5

18. Lisa C. Averyhart in Roghaar, *KnitLit*, 58.

19. *Navajo, Prairie*, and *Pacifica* are the names of Homespun yarns, manufactured by Lion Brand Yarn Company, New York.

20. Averyhart in *KnitLit*, 58–59.

21. Lydon, *Knitting Sutra*, 138–139.

CHAPTER 6

22. Lydon, *Knitting Sutra*, 137.

CHAPTER 7

23. Lydon, *Knitting Sutra*, 11.

24. Shulamith Oppenheim in *KnitLit*, 65.

25. Margaret Guenther, *The Practice of Prayer* (Cambridge, Mass.: Cowley Publications, 1998), 26.

26. Henri J. M. Nouwen, *Can You Drink the Cup?* (Notre Dame, Ind.: Ave Maria Press, 1996), 95.

27. Thomas Merton, *New Seeds of Contemplation* (New York: New Directions Books, 1961), 3.

CHAPTER 8

28. Nouwen, 58.

29. Myers, 154.

30. Sue Monk Kidd, "A Story-Shaped Life." *Weavings*, Spring 1989, 19–26.

CHAPTER 10

31. Rumi, *Rumi: In the Arms of the Beloved*. Translations by Jonathan Star (New York: Jeremy P. Tarcher/Putnam, 1997), 31.

32. Thich Nhat Hanh, *For a Future to be Possible: Commentaries on the Five Wonderful Precepts* (Berkeley, Calif.: Parallax Press, 1993).

33. Remen, *Kitchen Table Wisdom* (New York: Riverhead Books, 1996), 153.

CHAPTER 11

34. Loring, *Listening Spirituality*, 140.

35. Chaim Stern, ed., *Gates of Prayer for Shabbat and Weekdays* (New York: Central Conference of American Rabbis, 1994), 98.

36. David A. Teutsch, ed., *Kol Haneshamah-Shabbat Vehagim*, 3rd ed. (Elkins Park, Pa.: The Reconstructionist Press, 1996), 142.

CHAPTER 12

37. Elie Wiesel, *The Gates of the Forest: A Novel*. (New York: Schocken Books, 1995), 10.

38. Kidd, "A Story-Shaped Life," 25.

REFERENCES

Books and Articles

Burghardt, Walter. "Contemplation: A Long, Loving Look at the Real." *Church*, Winter 1989, 14–18.

Chittister, Joan. *A Passion for Life: Fragments of the Face of God*. Maryknoll, N.Y.: Orbis Books, 1996.

Goodall, Jane. *Reason for Hope: A Spiritual Journey*. New York: Warner Books, 2000.

Guenther, Margaret. *The Practice of Prayer*. Cambridge, Mass.: Cowley Publications, 1998.

Hanh, Thich Nhat. *For a Future to Be Possible: Commentaries on the Five Wonderful Precepts*. Berkeley, Calif.: Parallax Press, 1993.

Kidd, Sue Monk. "A Story-Shaped Life." *Weavings*, Spring 1989, 19–26.

David A. Teutsch, ed., *Kol Haneshamah-Shabbat Vehagim*, 3rd ed. Elkins Park, Pa.: The Reconstructionist Press, 1996.

Loring, Patricia. *Listening Spirituality: Volume I, Personal Spiritual Practices Among Friends*. Washington, D.C.: Openings Press, 1997.

Lydon, Susan Gordon. *The Knitting Sutra*. San Francisco: HarperSanFrancisco, 1997.

Main, John, O.S.B. *Moment of Christ: The Path of Meditation*. New York: Continuum Publishing Company, 1999.

Meister Eckhart: A Modern Translation. Translated by Raymond Blakney. New York: Harper & Row, Harper Torchbooks, 1941.

Merton, Thomas. *New Seeds of Contemplation*. New York: New Directions Books, 1961.

Myers, Lisa R. *The Joy of Knitting*. Philadelphia: Running Press, 2001.

Newman, Lewis, ed. *Hasidic Anthology*. New York: Schocken Books, 1963.

Nouwen, Henri J. M. *Can You Drink the Cup?* Notre Dame, Ind.: Ave Maria Press, 1996.

Remen, Rachel Naomi, M.D. *Kitchen Table Wisdom*. New York: Riverhead Books, 1996.

Roghaar, Linda, and Molly Wolf, eds. *KnitLit: Sweaters and Their Stories . . . and Other Writing About Knitting*. New York: Three Rivers Press, 2002.

Rumi. *Rumi: In the Arms of the Beloved*. Translated by Jonathan Star. New York: Jeremy P. Tarcher/Putnam, 1997.

Stern, Chaim, ed. *Gates of Prayer for Shabbat and Weekdays*. New York: Central Conference of American Rabbis, 1994.

Weisel, Elie. *The Gates of the Forest: A Novel*. New York: Schocken Books, 1995.

Websites

www.knittingintothemystery.com. Our website.

www.shawlministry.com. Official website of the shawl-knitting ministry.

www.silentwitness.net: Knit shawls for victims of domestic violence as a way to honor Sheila Wellstone.

ABOUT OUR CONTRIBUTORS

Janet Bristow is a 1997 graduate of the Women's Leadership Institute, Hartford Seminary, Hartford, Connecticut, and a member of their Alumni Council. She is the cofounder of the shawl ministry and coordinator of the prayer-shawl ministry at St. Patrick/St. Anthony Church, Hartford. Janet facilitates prayer-shawl workshops and red-tent experiences.

Kathleen O'Connell Chesto is an educator, storyteller, and retreat director who captivates her listeners with her insights on the holiness of ordinary life gleaned from her experience as a wife and mother. She holds a doctorate in ministry from Hartford Seminary and has received numerous awards for her work with families and for her books and videos.

Victoria A. Cole-Galo, the cofounder of the shawl ministry, is a graduate of the Women's Leadership Institute at the Hartford Seminary. Vicky is self-employed and married to the love of her life. She lives with her husband and two sons in Berlin, Connecticut.

Philip Goldberg, Ph.D., is a spiritual counselor and interfaith minister in Los Angeles. His most recent books are *Making Peace with God* (J. P. Tarcher) and *Roadsigns: Navigating Your Path to Spiritual Happiness* (Rodale Books). His website is www.philipgoldberg.com.

Kent Ira Groff, Ph.D., is founder and director of Oasis Ministries for Spiritual Development, Camp Hill, Pennsylvania. He is author of *The Soul of Tomorrow's Church: Weaving Spiritual Practices in Ministry Together* (Upper Room) and *What Would You Believe if You Didn't Believe Anything? A Handbook for Spiritual Orphans* (Jossey-Bass), along with other books, articles, poems, and hymns.

Rachel Harris, Ph.D., is a psychotherapist in private practice and the author of *20-Minute Retreats* (Owl Books).

Marye Gail Harrison is a spiritual director affiliated with the Spiritual Life Center in Bloomfield, Connecticut. She is an active Unitarian Universalist concerned about how we connect with one another and the whole earth. Retired from corporate training work, she occasionally writes poems and creates collages as she continues her spiritual journey.

Robert A. Jonas is the director of the Empty Bell, a Christian/Buddhist sanctuary near Boston (www.emptybell.org). He is a writer, spiritual companion, musician, and retreat leader. He is the author of *Henri Nouwen* (Orbis Books). His CDs, *Blowing Bamboo* and *New Life from Ruins*, are available at cdfreedom.com/robertjonas.

Kay Lindahl is the author of *The Sacred Art of Listening: Forty Reflections for Cultivating a Spiritual Practice* (Skylight Paths) and founder of the Listening Center in Laguna Niguel, California. She has been knitting on and off since she was nine years old and has recently rediscovered the joy and blessing of knitting.

Felicia B. McKnight is a Jungian spiritual director in private practice in Narragansett, Rhode Island. She writes, trains interns in spiritual direction, and presents expressive arts retreats with For the Love of Living™. Felicia has a coast-to-coast family that includes four daughters and two granddaughters.

Cathleen O'Meara Murtha is a Daughter of Wisdom (DW) dedicated to promoting wholeness and healing in individuals, communities, and in our world through spiritual growth and empowerment. At present she works at the Spiritual Life Center in Bloomfield, Connecticut, where she shares the wonders of the shawl-knitting ministry with others.

Susan Rakoczy, IHM, Ph.D. is a theologian, writer, and spiritual director. She is a member of the faculty of St. Joseph's Theological Institute, Cedara, South Africa, and has published in the areas of spirituality and feminist theology.

Anna and Monte Sugarman are rabbis, musicians, and the spiritual leaders of "Synagogue Without Walls, Or Chadash," in Ballston Spa, New York. They officiate at interfaith and nondenominational weddings and life-cycle events. They reach out to Jews and members of all faiths, regardless of affiliation, to promote an interfaith dialogue.

Brother Wayne Teasdale is a Christian *sannyasi* (monk) in the lineage of Bede Griffiths, O.S.B. Cam. He is an adjunct professor at Catholic Theological Union, DePaul University, and Columbia College in Chicago, and serves on the board of the Parliament of the World's Religions. He is the author of *The Mystic Heart* and *A Monk in the World* (New World Library).

Loretta Watts, a pastel artist who earned her M.F.A. in writing from Vermont College, has published poems in *The Best Spiritual Writing 2000* (Harper SanFrancisco), *Yankee Magazine, First Things,* and other journals. Presently leading workshops and finishing her first book, she lives in Connecticut with her husband.

Knitting Your Shawl

1. *Decide the size needle you will use.* Size 11 (8) will create a slightly denser shawl and the K3 pattern will be more noticeable. Conversely, size 13 (9) will create a slightly looser, less definable pattern. Approximate finished sizes, not counting fringe, are 26" x 60" on size 11 (66 cm x 152 cm on 8) needles and 30" x 64" on 13 (76 cm x 162 cm on 9) needles.

2. *Select your yarn.* You might pick a yarn for its color, for its texture, or for its name. Most shawls can be knit with three skeins of yarn that are six ounces (170 g) and 185 yards (166.5 m) each. If you prefer a larger shawl, you will need more yarn.

3. *Cast on.* Cast on 57 stitches for size 13 (9) needles, 63 for size 11 (8). The pattern is K3, P3 every row. This means that you will always begin with K3 and end with K3. Any odd multiple of three will work for your shawl, depending on how wide you want to make it: 57, 63, 69, 75, 81, and so on. Follow this pattern until you achieve the desired length. You may also decide to knit every row in what is called a *garter stitch*. **Before you begin the third skein, make your fringe.**

   A lap blanket for men is an alternative. In this case, you will cast on 87 stitches (size 13 (9)). This will give you a blanket that is approximately 45" (114cm) wide. You may want to use four skeins for this project.

4. *Make fringe.* Fringe is an individual thing. It can be long or short. You can put a piece of fringe through every stitch, or you can skip several stitches. Some people tie or sew beads to fringe, especially if the shawl is for a child. Whatever you decide, here is what you do:

   Decide how long you want the fringe. Because the fringe is doubled when you fasten it to the shawl, you must cut the fringe twice the desired length. For 6" (15 cm) fringe, each strand must be 12" (30 cm) long; for 12" fringe, cut pieces 24" (60 cm), and so on.

   For standard fringe, cut as many lengths as you have stitches on your needles. Reserve fringe until you have finished knitting the shawl.

5. *Finish the shawl.* Attach the inside end of the yarn to your shawl and continue knitting until all the yarn is used up, or until you have achieved the desired length.

6. *Attach the fringe.* Double the yarn and, using a small crochet hook, pull the loop through the stitch; insert the ends of the fringe through the loop and pull tight, creating a knot.

7. *Knot the ends of the fringe.* If you are using a yarn that frays easily, consider knotting the ends of the fringe.

8. *Give away your shawl.* If you are making the shawl for a particular person, you may want to include the history of the shawl ministry and a prayer. Many people wrap the shawl in tissue, include a sachet and a written blessing or prayer, and tie it with a leftover piece of yarn.

If you do not know a person who might need or want a shawl, check with churches and community groups in your area. They may know of people in need.

This text is adapted by Susan S. Jorgensen from the original by Victoria A. Cole-Galo and Janet Bristow © 2002. All rights reserved.

About Shawls . . .

The word "shawl" comes into the English language in 1662, from the Persian word *shAl*.

> Shawls have been made for centuries;
> they are universal and embracing;
> they comfort and enfold; wrap and warm;
> mother and hug; shelter and beauty.
> those who knit and receive shawls are loved and blessed.

A group of women who participated in the first Women's Leadership Institute at Hartford Seminary, Hartford, Connecticut, began this shawl-knitting ministry in 1998. Vicky Galo started knitting shawls for women who were undergoing treatment for breast cancer and other illnesses; Janet Bristow started knitting shawls for new mothers. Other members of the Institute began knitting shawls for their friends, family members, and people who just needed a shawl.

People knit shawls for many different reasons. Shawls celebrate birthdays and anniversaries, friendship and love, and professional and personal achievements. If one could wear the heartfelt sentiments often found in a greeting card, it would be as a shawl. Shawls console those who are grieving, comfort those who are ill, bring hope to those who are in despair. Parents knit shawls for their children; children knit shawls for aging parents. The reasons to knit a shawl are as numerous as the people who knit and receive them.

Cathy Murtha, a Daughter of Wisdom and director of the Spiritual Life Center in Bloomfield, Connecticut, introduced this ministry to many people at the Spiritual Life Center. Cathy creates Wisdom Mantles for marking significant passages in women's lives when they claim their unique gift of Wisdom.

Susan S. Izard, a United Church of Christ minister at First Church in West Hartford, Connecticut, wrote an article about this shawl-knitting ministry for *Presence: The Journal of Spiritual Directors International* in September 2000. As a result, people all over the world are knitting and receiving these wonderful gifts of love.

This ministry continues to grow. When you wear your shawl, you are connected with many people throughout the world. May you knit the shawl you give away with love, may you be blessed by the shawls that you knit and receive, and may you extend that blessing to those you love.